ADULTING
Like a
BOSS

Your grown-up survival guide

LAURA THOMAE YOUNG

ADULTING Like a BOSS

Your grown-up survival guide

LAURA THOMAE YOUNG

Would you like a FREE audio version?

Read This First

Just to say thanks for buying my book, I would like to give you the audio version 100% FREE!

To Download Go To:

www.AdultingLikeABoss.net/audiobook

WHAT PEOPLE ARE SAYING

I find the advice in Adulting Like a Boss *relatable and applicable! Wonderful book.*
— Paula Kay

Laura Thomae Young's down to earth words are full of practicality, wisdom and humor. From how to find a decent group of friends to taking care of your body, budget and car, each chapter holds a game plan anyone can follow!
— Edith Kennedy

This book is extremely relatable! I just got married, so now I'm trying to do "adulty" things like combine bank accounts and buy a house!
— Anna Miller

Laura Thomae Young...you've got something really AMAZING here!
— Vannesia Darby

I will definitely have my grown and near-grown children read it. This book is a keeper!
— Anne Young

Reading this book should be a graduation requirement! I love the book, and am finding lots of inspiration and wonderful quotes.
— Alison Smith

I identified with the book from the very first chapter. I have felt unprepared for adult life, but maybe part of Adulting is learning what you don't know, and asking the right questions. Thank goodness for this book to get me started.
— Mary Kathryn Lunceford-Levesque

Adulting Like a Boss *is a great "How To" book for life. It's a must read even if you think you have 'Adulting' down. Thanks, Laura Thomae Young, for your no-nonsense approach.*
– Martha Hennessey

I wish I had something like this when I was fresh out of school. This is literally a hand guide for making grown-up decisions! It's very easy to follow, and I feel like Laura Thomae Young is talking to me as I read.
– Christina Dotson

This book is a practical guide for those beginning to walk out into the world of independence. Laura Thomae Young has opened her heart to share her life experiences and wisdom.
– Cindy Mount

Reading the chapter on finances made me look to see if I really understand what money is taken out of my paycheck. Now I have some questions for HR when I go back to work next week!
– Kristin Guest

Adulting Like a Boss *would be a great graduation gift! I love the chapter on being positive. It's even a great reminder for those of us who have been "Adulting" for a couple of decades.*
– Abby Huffman

Written with subtle humor and full of wisdom, Adulting Like a Boss *is easy to read and flows smoothly. The practical examples give everything you need in one place – the what, why, and how.*
– Lynn Naughton

The best way I can describe this book is—It's the book I didn't know I needed but SO glad I have now.
– Duaa Elnasri

*To my mom, who taught me how to
Adult Like a Boss, and asked me every
day how my book was coming.*

Copyright © 2017 by Laura Thomae Young
All rights reserved under International and Pan-American Copyright Conventions. This book or any portion thereof may not be reproduced or used in any manner whatsoever without the express written permission of the publisher except for the use of brief quotations in a book review.

First Printing, 2017

ISBN-13: 978-1977950314
ISBN-10: 1977950310

Editor: Michelle Chalkey (http://michellechalkey.com)
Author Photo: McKenzie Stephens w/ Kenzie Stephens Photography (https://kenziestephensphotography.com)

Published by: YesBear Publishing

www.facebook.com/AdultingLikeABoss

www.AdultingLikeABoss.net

Author available for speaking and training

CONTACT INFO:
Laura Thomae Young with *Adulting Like a Boss!*
laura@Adultinglikeaboss.net

CONTENTS

Introduction	11
1. Why is it So Hard to Be a Grown-Up?	17
2. It's the Hard Things That Make Life Easy	25
3. Adulting the Deep Life	41
4. Adulting with Your Best Self	47
5. Adulting with Positivity	55
6. Adulting Through Meaningful Work	67
7. Adulting with Your Decisions	75
8. Adulting Means Taking Care of Yourself	81
9. Adulting with Your Health	89
10. Adulting with Your Money	101
11. Adulting with Your Taxes	117
12. Adulting Like a Homeowner – The Money Part	129
13. Adulting Like a Homeowner – The House Part	143
14. Adulting with Your Time	151
15. Adulting with the Right Habits	161
16. Adulting Over and Over	179
17. Adulting for Building New Friendships	193
18. Adulting to Beat Your Excuses	199
Conclusion	211

How To's

Sew on a Button	**38**
Volunteer Like a Boss!	**64**
Host a Party at Home **that Everyone Talks About for Weeks**	**98**
Find a Bargain and Save Money **on Everyday Purchases**	**115**
Boil a Perfect Egg That's Neither Gooey nor Green	**141**
Take Care of Your Car	**176**
Do Your Laundry **Without Ruining All Your Clothes!**	**189**
Check Your Car's Tire Pressure	**207**

A classic book is a book everyone wishes
they had already read.

— Laura Thomae Young

INTRODUCTION

"Be warned that I am bossy and nosy and I love asking questions and giving advice and getting all up in your business. But know that I am also in love with life and enraptured with people."

--LAURA THOMAE YOUNG, AUTHOR

Adulting equals commitment.

Following through. A job well done. Seeing it through from start to finish.

Taking responsibility. Doing the Hard Thing when you don't want to.

Adulting means stepping up to the plate, and with your best effort, swinging at a ball that's coming faster and harder than you are ready for.

Adulting is hard because you don't get a participation trophy. You won't get told what a special snowflake you are at your job unless you work your tail off, and even then, you may not get noticed.

Adulting means paying your bills on time. Sticking with a job you don't like because you know it's making you grow. It's using your hard-earned money to buy a lawnmower, or fix the dishwasher instead of taking a trip to the beach. It's bringing your own lunch and getting up early every day to fix it rather than picking up something at the drive through.

Gee, I'm making it sound like it's all effort and no fun, and that's definitely not true. I'm NOT here to tout the "life's hard and then you die" philosophy.

Adulting is also freedom. Not freedom *from* responsibility, rather freedom *through* responsibility.

For the first time in your life, you get to choose your own path. You get to decide every day what you're going to do with the next twenty-four hours, the next week, the next month, and the next year.

You are free from parents and teachers *making* you do stuff. Instead, you have the freedom to choose what stuff you'll do.

This is the time in your life when you get to write your own story. You can learn and grow and meet new people and make decisions all on your own. The world is your oyster, as Shakespeare put it, to open up and grab the pearl.

My purpose for this book is two-fold. First is to motivate you to live your life to its fullest. Take full advantage of the opportunity you have – time, energy, youth, brains, and your uniqueness – and don't settle on a life of mediocrity.

Introduction

Secondly, there are skills I have found that millennials have somehow missed learning, and I'd like to teach you a few practical life lessons. Some are the simple *how-to's* you'll find scattered throughout the book, and some are built right into the chapters.

It's important that you know something about me right up front: Be warned that I am bossy and nosy and I love asking questions and giving advice and getting all up in your business.

> **Adulting is also freedom. Not freedom from responsibility, rather freedom through responsibility.**

But know that I am also in love with life and enraptured with people. I love all kinds of people. I love the freshness of a new baby, and the persistence of a two-year-old. I love sitting and listening to octogenarians and nonagenarians (fancy words for folks in their eighties and nineties) share the wisdom of their years. My husband's great-grandmother once told me, "Honey, there's a lot you don't know." And she's right! The more I know, the more I know there's much to learn.

Most of all, though, I particularly seem to be drawn to twenty-somethings. I think it's because I am energized by the vigor of youth and the anticipation of a life just starting to be discovered and lived. I love to see the future laid out, choosing this path or that with excitement, some fear and trepidation, and boundless energy for forging ahead. The twenties are the years when so many important decisions are made – career, home, romance, family. It's scary and exciting and loads of fun.

I've found myself working with teens and twenty-somethings in some capacity all throughout my adult life. I've mentored, discipled, taught, laughed with, and cried with hundreds of young people through the years. In large groups, I find myself ditching the folks my age in order to sit and listen to the hopes, dreams, and accomplishments of those just starting out in life.

I come to you with some experience - some coming from my own victories and failures and some coming from the stories and experiences of others I have known.

I am here to tell you what I think. I am here to offer advice.

In our family, we have a saying of "yah'-dah" – which is colloquial "you ought to." I don't want to say, "you ought to" or "you should," but I can't help myself! I see potential in you! I see opportunity. It's exciting for me to share with you the wisdom I've gained from doing lots of things wrong and a few things right. I figured some of it out myself, was taught some of it by my amazing parents, and learned more than my fair share through failures...and a little bit through victories too.

So...let's get Adulting.

Doing the hard thing is walking across the room to put things away, even when you don't feel like it.

— Laura Thomae Young

– 1 –
WHY IS IT SO HARD TO BE A GROWN-UP?

"The transition from college to Adulting is an even greater jump than it was from high school to college. Everything is upside down!"

Adulting = Pressure

The pressure starts with the famous question, "What do you want to be when you grow up?"

Then later, if you're college bound, the question becomes, "What are you going to major in?"

And suddenly, you arrive at adulthood! You pass your twenty-first birthday. No longer a teen, out on your own, college or vocational training behind you, and voila! You're grown up – so what are you?

Now you're trying to figure out "Adulting," and the main thing you're finding is that you don't know how to do it. There are things you think you should know how to do, but you don't. There are things you're not doing that you're afraid you should be doing. You feel ill-equipped and ill-prepared.

There's pressure to "adult" and you're not sure you're ready. I mean, wasn't somebody supposed to teach you *how*?

You feel like there are gaps in your education.

You know how to find the square root of a number, but don't know how to cook a meal.

> **There's pressure to "adult" and you're not sure you're ready. I mean, wasn't somebody supposed to teach you *how*?**

You can recite the preamble to the Constitution, but aren't sure how to register to vote or get involved in local elections.

You landed a job in your career and are making a salary, but don't know how to make a budget or pay bills on time.

And don't get me started on taxes. What the heck is *that* all about, right? Why are they so complicated? And you mean to tell me that if you don't pay your taxes you can actually go to jail, but nobody taught you how to do it? Wouldn't *that* have been a good class to have in high school or college?

Why is it So Hard To Be a Grown-up?

And on and on it goes. Housing - do you rent or buy? Post-college relationships - how the heck do you meet people? Office politics? Ugh, what's that all about?

Why didn't anybody tell you it was gonna be so COMPLICATED? You somehow pictured it being, well...easier.

There's pressure to "make a difference" and "live your dreams," but you're not even sure what that means for you. Getting a job, settling down, paying bills, hanging out with friends - is any of that really living the dream?

Adulting is different than college life, and the transition from college to Adulting is an even greater jump than it was from high school to college. Everything is upside down.

> *I am looking at my bank account after a bachelorette weekend, paying six months of car insurance, listening to the auto-mechanic tell me everything that needs to be replaced on my car, calling the natural gas company about a gas leak at my house, changing the home rental insurance policy address after my move, and paying more for a bridesmaid's dress to be hemmed than the actual cost of the dress....yeah ...I'm Adulting....and I don't like it!*
>
> *--Emily T – 25*

In school, A+B=C – but now… you don't even know what the problem is to solve. You aren't sure where to find A and B, much less if they equal C.

School gave clear expectations and clear *goals*. School gave structure. School gave activities to meet people and easily form friendships.

But now? The expectations aren't all that clear and you're not sure you're meeting them.

You have new and unfamiliar responsibilities - adult responsibilities - and you don't know what to do. There's no syllabus, no outline to follow. You feel like you have to figure it out on your own. Play it by ear as you go.

And then there's pressure by society to have it all together. You feel that the expectation is that you should be on your career path, in a relationship, and have your life set out before you. But you don't, and you play the what-if game in your head. What if this is the wrong career? The wrong relationship? The wrong town?

> **Don't compare your behind-the-scenes with someone else's highlights reel.**

In high school or college, a wrong decision may have had consequences, but not like they do now. The stakes are higher as an adult.

The clock has started! Relationships - gotta settle down and have children, right? Career – gotta land the "dream job!" Money? Pay the bills. Pinch the pennies. Save for retirement. Give to charity. These kinds of decisions have repercussions that will follow you for years.

Pressure!

I certainly don't claim to have it all figured out, but I have noticed some trends as I've talked to lots of twenty-somethings:

- There really are some gaps – things you need to know that you should have learned, but were never taught.
- Some of it is actually hard and the millennials didn't think that things were going to be hard.
- It takes time and nobody likes that. We live in an instant world and things that take time suck.
- It means getting out of your comfort zone and that sucks too.
- Life is more complex than it ever has been, and there are things you have to deal with that your parents and grandparents didn't.
- There's pressure to live your dreams and make your mark and create a legacy.
- Competition is fierce and you have to work hard to rise above the noise and be noticed.
- We worship celebrity, and social media makes everyone feel they should be celebrity-like.
- Limiting beliefs hold you back.
- Adulting appears to some as all work and no play, making it unappealing.

Social media makes it look like everyone has it all together, but after talking to dozens of millennials just like you – out of college, on their own, trying to "adult," I can assure you that nobody has it all figured out.

Don't let pictures and sound bites on Facebook, Instagram, and Snapchat fool you. Everybody is struggling to figure life out. That's not what people post on social media, though. They don't show you the struggle – only the good parts.

Don't compare your behind-the-scenes with someone else's highlights reel.

Obviously one chapter, one lecture, one book of how-to's isn't going to prepare you for Adulting, but the next few chapters will equip you with answers for some of the questions you may be asking and some of the things you didn't even know you needed to know.

Doing the hard thing...it's gonna hurt like heck —
but then it's gonna be great!

— Laura Thomae Young

– 2 –
IT'S THE HARD THINGS THAT MAKE LIFE EASY

"It seems like hard = hard.
But hard = better now and easier down the road."

All throughout the book, I'm going to talk about doing "the Hard Thing." The Hard Thing is the option you may not want to do, but you know is the right thing to do. It's the thing you do NOW that ultimately will make life easier down the road.

Doing the Hard Thing is…. well….. hard. It's often unpleasant. It takes more strength than you really want to expend.

But once it's done, there's benefit and reward.

When you do the Hard Thing – even when you don't want to, *especially* when you don't want to – it ultimately makes life easier, and oftentimes *better*.

It's counter-intuitive. It seems like hard = hard. But hard = better now and easier down the road.

> **The hard thing is the option you may not want to do, but you know is the right thing to do. It's the thing you do NOW that ultimately will make life easier down the road.**

Besides the reward of having accomplished the "whatever-it-is-that-needs-doing-and-you-have-to-suck-it-up-and-just-do," there's another reward. It's the ooey-gooey good feeling that comes from doing the Hard Thing.

There's a positive intrinsic value that begins at your nose and seeps down to your toes. It's the "I'm-so-proud-of-myself-for-Adulting!" feeling that you get.

We hear a lot about self-esteem – about the importance of building up your self-esteem and not having low self-esteem - but there's not much out there that tells us HOW to build it up.

Yes, you're special. Yes, you're wonderful. Yes, you're loved. And we definitely get our value from who we are and not what we do.

But…there's something magical that happens when you do the Hard Thing – the RIGHT thing.

It feels good.

It's the Hard Things That Make Life Easy

It feels good and it makes you proud of yourself, and your self-esteem gets a little boost.

Do that enough times and the accumulation of those positive feelings leads to a positive self-image and knowledge that you're doing the right thing.

Let's take volunteering in your community, for example. That's a very "Adulty" thing to do, right?

But it's hard. You have to find out what's available, and then you have to find out how and where to sign up, and then you have to make the commitment to be in a certain place at a certain time. And then you second-guess yourself because what if you don't like it, or nobody but you shows up, and yada-yada-yada – you nearly talk yourself out of the whole idea.

> But...there's something magical that happens when you do the hard thing – the RIGHT thing.

But let's say you find out that there's a group who is building a garden in the inner city. You hear about it from a friend, make the effort to sign up (Hard Thing), put it on your calendar (a little hard), AND you find out you have to bring gardening gloves and a spade (also hard, because where in the heck do you buy those things and what is a spade anyway?).

But you do it. You sign up, buy the things you need at a hardware store, (by the way a spade is a hand-held shovel), get up early on Saturday, drive across town, and ta-da, the battle is half-won. Your self-esteem gets a boost because you chose to show up rather than sleep another hour and miss it altogether.

Now is the real reward. The good stuff. You work all day (physical exercise), outdoors (you're always in an office and haven't seen the sun in weeks). You and your friend spend the day together, meet lots of new people – people who care about their community – PLUS you've done a really good thing. You've served your community. The truth is, as you may have heard before, doing a good thing for someone else often helps the giver as much or more than the receiver.

You did something helpful for your community. It feels good. It *is* good. YOU are good.

Enough of those experiences and you'll find that the responsibility you've just taken leads to two things: maturity (you're Adulting!) and positive self-esteem.

Adulting isn't all about making yourself feel good, though. It's about choosing to do the Hard Thing when you reaaaallllllyyyy don't want to. It's about taking responsibility when you'd rather not.

Responsibility is a surprising path to freedom

It seems that freedom *from* responsibility should be what leads to freedom. How can it be that taking responsibility gives us real freedom?

In the 1960s, when the Hippie movement came about, this new counter-culture was about not being weighed down by responsibilities. The youth of the day saw their parents trudging along, under the "yoke" of responsibility, confined by jobs at factories, paying mortgages, and living under a burdensome yoke of tradition.

So the youth of the day rebelled and the days of "free love" and "make love not war" were born. They wanted to do their own thing. But within a few years, the freedom they wanted wasn't there. Where were they ten years later? Working responsible jobs. Paying mortgages. In monogamous marriages. The "free love" wasn't so free after all. And "doing your own thing" had often meant not doing ANYthing, and they found that that was no way to live.

> **Enough of those experiences and you'll find that the responsibility you've just taken leads to two things: maturity (you're Adulting!) and positive self-esteem.**

I'm definitely not ditching the whole movement, because there were many good things that our society gained from those years - tie-dyed shirts, for example, and some amazing music.

I think they thought that the life of responsibility – Adulting life – was boring. And I think that the idea has resurfaced with millennials. But life doesn't have to be boring! It *shouldn't* be boring.

I want to be very clear on this: It isn't freedom from responsibility that makes life boring; It's responsibility that makes an exciting life possible.

Doing the Hard Thing = Responsibility. Responsibility = Maturity. Maturity = Adulting. Like a Boss.

A three-minute rule

Do you know about the five-second rule?

It's a ridiculous rule that many people use – that if you drop something on the floor and it is there for less than five seconds, it didn't have time to gather any germs, so it is fine to eat.

This isn't that.

This is a three-minute rule, and it doesn't involve eating anything off the floor.

The three-minute rule is taking any task – any Adulting thing – that you don't particularly want to do (the Hard Thing) and either doing it or preparing to do it in three minutes. You can also turn this into the One-Minute rule, or the Ten-Minute rule, or even the One-Hour rule. Set an amount of time that you think you can stick with, and time yourself. But for the sake of this chapter, we're going to use the Three-Minute rule.

I suggest using an actual timer. If you don't already have one on your phone (hint: it's in the same place you have an alarm,) you can download an app. But do absolutely use a timer – an egg timer, your phone, or a song that lasts three minutes.

> **Just do it and it will be DONE!**

You aren't going to WANT to do it

The three-minute rule is for anything that you don't *want* to do, but know you *should* do. The Adulting thing that is nagging at you, or making your life HARD because you've chosen the EASY way.

Have you seen the show Unbreakable Kimmy Schmidt? *It's a show about a group of girls who were held captive in an underground bunker and told that the world had ended. There was a crank they had to turn constantly, and Kimmy made a game of it. If I can just turn it while I count to ten, she would say, and then another ten and another.*

You can do almost anything for three minutes, even the most unpleasant of tasks. Even the scary things. Even the Adult-y things you don't know how to do or don't want to do.

But before you start, let's figure out what it is that's holding you back

Is it really a priority? Is this something you think you should do, but isn't really important? Is it something that can wait? Is it something that could go undone?

If the answer to these is Nope, then ask yourself this: Is there a limiting belief that's holding me back?

I'm not good enough. I'm not smart enough. What if I fail? Everyone else knows how but me.

Write those limiting beliefs out, tell yourself how ridiculous they are, and move on. They're probably not true. You ARE good enough. You ARE smart enough. And if you fail? So what! Get up, try again, and keep going! You are Super Woman! You are Adulting Like a Boss!

Take three minutes

Three minutes seems like a short time, but it's actually amazing how much you can get done with full-on focus for three minutes. If you don't think three minutes is a long time, set a timer. Stand up wherever you are

– yes you have to actually put the book down – and do jumping jacks for three minutes. Unless you're in pretty decent physical shape, those short three minutes seem really looooong.

Now let's see what you can get done in three long minutes.

You can:

- **Get it done completely** – Yep. Just do it and it will be DONE. What can you do in three minutes? Pick up all your clothes and start a load of laundry. Read a page of a book. Answer an email. Clean off the countertop. Check your bank balance. Write a thank-you note to your Aunt Martha for the birthday money. Make your bed. Check the oil in your car. Make a dentist appointment. Pack a lunch for work.

- **Get started** – Not everything Adult-y can be accomplished in three minutes, but you can at least get it started. Use the three minutes to do Step One. Look up one recipe to cook for dinner. Get your car manual out and find the place in the back where it tells you what maintenance should be done. Make an appointment with a mortgage lender to find out about buying a house. You don't have to finish. Just get started.

- **Organize yourself or your stuff to get it done** – You may need a few things to do this Hard Thing. Use the three-minute rule to make a list of what you need, or gather up what you need. Or order what you need to be delivered. Or get everything ready to do the Hard Thing. You may find that getting the supplies or lists or whatever it is you need can all be done in three minutes.

- **Learn how** – Use the three minutes to watch a video on "how to." Learn how to check the oil in your car. Learn how to prepare the dish you're planning on cooking. Don't let not knowing how hold you back. Order a book, sign up for a course, or enroll in a class.

- **Learn how to start** – If your Hard Thing is too much to learn how to do completely, you can at least learn what the first step is, and either do it, or prepare to do it. Just knowing how to even start is a good step and will get you moving in the right direction.

Momentum — once you get started

Have you ever been working on a project and lost all track of time? It's the momentum. The hard part is the starting. But once you get going, you find that it's not so hard to KEEP going.

If you've been putting something off and you use the three-minute rule, you may find that you spend more than three minutes doing it. Often it's just the STARTING part that's hard. That's why there's so much magic in the three-minute rule. Even though you tell yourself you only have to do it for three minutes – you can either stop, or keep going.

> **The hard part is the starting. But once you get going, you find that it's not so hard to KEEP going.**

But give yourself a maximum – especially if it's an unpleasant task. Because you're likely to not ever come back to it if it goes on too long and is a negative experience.

Try – No less than three. No more than ten. Use a timer and set it for three minutes. If you're still involved in your project, and aren't ready to quit, set it for seven more minutes, for a maximum of ten minutes.

Helpful Hints

Do you find yourself fizzling out? You start but you don't finish? You do three minutes but then you never get back to it? You bargain with yourself, but you let yourself off the hook? Here are a couple of ways to get moving again:

Be brave.

If you know something is going to only last three minutes, would you risk feeling weird, awkward, or uncomfortable to get it done? Would you call the mechanic or the dentist or the accountant if you promised yourself you would only feel dorky for three minutes? Be brave! Take the big plunge into the unknown – for only three minutes.

Pretend.

When you are ready to do your Hard Thing but you lack the confidence, here's a simple exercise to try.

For three minutes, pretend you are the most responsible Adult you know. Ask yourself, "Who is the Adultiest Adult who would do this Like a Boss? How would they do it?"

> It's much more difficult to back-pedal once you've announced to the world that you are going to DO THIS THING!

Now, pretend for three minutes that you are that person. Pretend you're confident even if you don't feel confident. Pretend you're an expert even if you feel like a novice. You are an Adult. And for three minutes, do the Hard Thing.

Make it public.

Announce that you are going to do this hard, Adult-y thing. You can announce it on Facebook, Instagram, or Snapchat, but let other people know you are plunging into the big adult world with this Hard Thing, and that you are starting with three minutes. See how much traction you get in three minutes. You may want to keep giving yourself three- to ten-minute deadlines until it is all done, but either way, let everyone know. It's much more difficult to back-pedal once you've announced to the world that you are going to DO THIS THING.

Give yourself a deadline.

Once you've done the first three minutes, you'll have momentum. Now give yourself a deadline (and this is where your accountability partner will really come in handy,) to finish the Hard Thing.

You found a dentist – so make an appointment before the end of the month.

You made a list of ingredients for a meal - so go to the grocery store, pick them up, and fix the meal by the end of the weekend.

You found a mechanic – so set a time you are going to take your car in to get fixed.

You gathered your gardening tools – so commit to when you are going to plant your flowers.

When you were in college, and a paper was due – whether you were the kind of person who had it done a week early or you pulled an all-nighter and got it in right on the dot, either way - you were working on a deadline.

One of the challenges with being an Adult is that there are important things you have to get done, but there's nobody setting a deadline for you. You have to set your own deadline.

Make a game of it.

Make it fun, make it challenging, make a game of it – whatever it takes for you to get moving toward your goals.

Are you a visual person? Do what you can see first.

Are you a list maker? See how many things you can knock out in three minutes.

> Perfect is the enemy of the good. Just DO it. For most things in life, DONE – even if it's not done perfectly, is better than something perfectly HALF done.

Race against the clock (or timer). See how many different things you can accomplish in three-minute batches.

One game I make for myself when tidying up is take a basket or box and go clockwise around the room, either picking up, tidying, dusting, or depositing things that need to be put away. Don't criss-cross the room – that's cheating.

Or I will only pick up one category of things – clothes, books, or toys (when you have little ones or fur babies).

Rewards for winning are good too! Food rewards (sweets) usually work for me, but that's not for everyone.

Better to DO it than PLAN to do it perfectly

As I was working on this book, I read somewhere, "Nobody cares as much about what you're PLANNING to do as they do about what is DONE." It was great motivation for me to keep going! FINISH the task. Do the Hard Thing.

Perfect is the enemy of the good. Just DO it. For most things in life, DONE – even if it's not done perfectly, is better than something perfectly HALF done.

Can you make do with what you have on hand? Do you really need to buy something to do your Hard Thing?

I'm a minimalist in my kitchen, and I've fed hundreds of people over the course of my adult life. But I don't have every single kitchen gadget. My mother-in-law, on the other hand, also feeds the masses with guests at her table multiple times a week, and she has two or three of every kitchen item that exists! We both love to cook and entertain, but for me, I don't like a lot of "stuff."

The point is, we can both make a great meal for a lot of people, but I can do it with just a few items. There are always ways to substitute, so don't let things like not having everything perfectly in place stop you from getting it done.

Don't let a perfect tool, perfect time, or perfect circumstances stop you. Just do it, then it will be done.

HOW TO...

Sew on a Button

If your favorite shirt is missing a button, it's easier than you might think to replace it!

What you'll need:

- Scissors
- A sewing needle
- Matching thread
- A button.

A couple of notes:

- If you still have the missing button, GREAT! If it's lost, check the inside of the garment around the hem and along the seams. Oftentimes the manufacturer will sew on extra buttons for replacements.
- If you don't have a button, most discount stores (like Walmart) will have a sewing section where you can buy buttons. Even most grocery stores have a small sewing kit with replacement buttons included. If you can't find your exact button, get a button similar in size and color. You can cut off one of the existing buttons from a part of the garment that doesn't show (much) and use the new unmatched button to replace it.

The Steps

1. Thread the needle with about 18" of thread. Pull the two ends until they are even, and tie a knot.
2. Start on the underside of the fabric and push the needle through, pulling it all the way until the knot is touching the fabric.
3. Thread the needle through the button until the button is in the right place.
    - If this is a four-holed button, from the top, go diagonally and push the needle back down through the opposite hole, pulling the thread all the way through. Now the button should have one

stitch and be in place. Repeat this about four times, taking care to go back and forth through the same place to make it look tidy on the bottom.

* Don't pull the thread super tight. You need the button to have a little wiggle room.

4. To give the button plenty of wiggle room so it will fit through the button hole, you'll now do a "shank" stitch. From the underside of the fabric, push the needle up underneath the button, but don't go through the holes of the button. Circle the button three times, wrapping the thread around the threads you've already sewn, between the button and the fabric. Then push the needle back through the fabric, underneath the button, to the underside of the fabric.
5. Now sew the other two holes of the button, repeating the process with four stitches.
6. To finish up, make a little stitch through some of the threads on the underside of the fabric and tie a knot. Clip the ends and ta-dah! You're done!

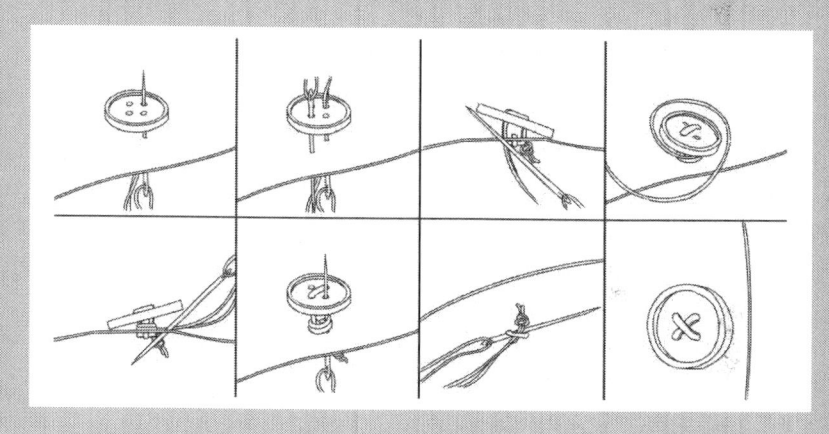

The good stuff comes from doing the hard thing.
— Laura Thomae Young

– 3 –

ADULTING THE DEEP LIFE

*"I don't want to just live or just survive each day
- I want to live big and live fully."*

All throughout the book, I'm going to talk about doing "the Hard Thing." The Hard Thing is the option you may not want to do, but you know is the right thing to do. It's the thing you do NOW that ultimately will make life easier down the road.

In his poem "Walden," Henry David Thoreau offers his deliberation on living deeply and purposefully.

> I went to the woods because I wished to live deliberately, to front only the essential facts of life, and see if I could not learn what it had to teach, and not, when I came to die, discover that I had not lived. I did not wish to live what was not life, living is so dear; nor

did I wish to practice resignation, unless it was quite necessary. *I wanted to live deep and suck out all the marrow of life*, to live so sturdily and Spartan-like as to put to rout all that was not life, to cut a broad swath and shave close, to drive life into a corner, and reduce it to its lowest terms, and, if it proved to be mean, why then to get the whole and genuine meanness of it, and publish its meanness to the world; or if it were sublime, to know it by experience, and be able to give a true account of it in my next excursion.

This poem was revitalized a few decades ago when Robin Williams' character John Keating, an English professor at a boarding school, teaches his apathetic students to "suck out the marrow" in the 1989 film *Dead Poets Society*.

For Thoreau, learning to suck the marrow of life meant moving into the woods and living simply. He wanted to strip life down to the basics and see what meaning he could derive from it.

> **Don't wait for the perfect time or the perfect circumstances. Don't settle, and don't give up too easily.**

I take the sucking-the-marrow phrase to mean maximizing every day and trying to get the most out of life. I want to go to bed tired every night, knowing that I have spent all the energy allotted to me for the day.

I don't want to just live or just *survive* each day - I want to live big and live fully. I want to create and dream and make things happen. I want to fill each day with meaningful work and life and love and laughter. I want to know more people and know people more.

I want to invest each minute of each day into a meaningful experience. I want to not dread Monday mornings and hope the day goes by quickly. I want to enjoy my work and the people I am with. If I am biding my time Monday through Friday, living only for a party on the weekend so I can forget my life and numb my sentiments of meaninglessness, then what kind of life is that?

We only get *one* life, one opportunity to fill it up.

Suck the marrow! Live big. Decide what your dream is and go for it. Don't wait for the perfect time or the perfect circumstances. Don't settle, and don't give up too easily. Once you've decided which path you're taking, follow it through. Don't quit when it gets hard; keep going! And unless it becomes painfully obvious early on that you're going in the wrong direction, give it time.

Finding Your Marrow

Let me give you an example from my life. I've been working in corporate America for seven years in a great company doing meaningful work, but still, I wanted something different – something bigger. I knew I loved writing, so I took a course on making a living doing creative writing for other people – blogs and sales copy, that sort of thing. I created a website, set everything up, and began pitching for jobs with potential clients. After a few months, I realized that I was going in the wrong direction. It wasn't fun and it wasn't fulfilling. I had an ache for something and I moved ahead, but quickly realized I was going in the wrong direction.

> I love the life I have, but I am creating the life I want. I don't have to choose one or the other.

Adulting Like a Boss

So I iterated and did some soul-searching. My life-coach husband and I spent a couple of days planning and thinking, crying and praying, and putting sticky notes all over the wall until I found something in the writing genre that was my passion. That's how the Adulting Like a Boss movement was born.

> *Adulting Like a Boss means paying my own medical bills, and paying them on time. Once I started paying for my own health insurance, I knew I was really a grown-up!*
>
> *--Ashley S – 25*

It's easier to steer a moving ship, they say, and that's exactly what happened with me. If I hadn't taken the writing course, I probably wouldn't be where I am today. Copywriting and ghostwriting for others was not the right direction for me, but it helped lead me down a path that facilitated me to find my calling. I had to do something, but it took doing the wrong thing to find the right thing.

If you're having a hard time finding what your marrow is, you may need to try different things. The more creative a person you are, the more iterations you may have. But choose something, stick with it for a time, and live life fully while you try it.

I love the life I have, but I am creating the life I want. I don't have to choose one or the other. I can love both – the present and the future I am creating - and so can you.

You can't let anyone else decide what your marrow is, because it's different for every person. But biding your time and doing activities that numb you rather than make you alive is a terrible waste.

Don't deprive the world of YOU. Whatever you're meant to do – what you can do and what you want to give to the world – is your marrow. Offer it. Give it. Live deliberately, as Thoreau tells us. Suck the marrow out of life.

Choose now or life will force you to choose later.

— Laura Thomae Young

– 4 –

ADULTING WITH YOUR BEST SELF

"Not tomorrow. Not next week or next month or next year. NOW is your time!"

My friend Maddie recently achieved her doctorate degree at age twenty-four. I'm impressed. According to Pew Research, only about fifty-six percent of students earn bachelor degrees within six years, and here's Maddie, passing up the crowds with a doctorate in the same amount of time.

What drives people like Maddie to achieve more in less time? I believe it is the drive to be the best version of themselves – to perform at the top of their game. Maddie is smart, talented, and driven to be her best, but she also knew what she wanted and went hard and fast after her goal.

> **It's the small daily steps that get you to your goal.**

Maddie walked across the stage of her university, diploma in hand, knowing that she had a couple of job offers waiting. She is now in the process of making sure she takes her time to get the right job that will allow her to offer her very best to the world. Maddie is constantly practicing and learning to become the best version of herself.

Determining your best self

The only person you need to compare yourself against is the "you" that you are capable of being. I know to measure myself against my own potential. I don't measure myself against a brain surgeon, or a ballerina, or even a writer and speaker who is much more accomplished or polished than I. I have a gift to give to the world – and it is myself.

Likewise, you have a gift to give to the world – and it is YOU. There is no one like you with your unique talents and gifts and experiences. The decision to be the best you has to start inside you. No one is going to come and pull it out – but the world will be ever so grateful when you offer it up.

You are capable of doing and being something wonderful. But if you use the excuse that it's too hard, and settle for something that's "pretty good," you will have wasted your unspent talent and deprived yourself and others of the something wonderful. If it's too hard or you don't know how you'll do it, you might never get started at all.

Here are three steps to help you become the best version of yourself:

1. **Decide what the best "you" looks like** – Even if you don't know *how* you're going to reach the goal of becoming what you can and want to be, set the goal. The path will present itself. Set your eyes on the horizon and start paddling.

2. **Get moving** – Nothing motivates like activity. Even when you don't feel like being your best, do it anyway. Get up early even when you're sleepy. Do the daily activities that get you to your goal even when you don't feel like it. Once you're moving, it's easier to stay moving. The hardest part is getting started.

3. **Work your tail off** – It takes lots and lots of work, done over a long period of time, to accomplish something wonderful. To become the very best version of YOU, you have to work at it every day, but the good news is, that once you start working hard every day, it becomes easier, and fun, and always always always worth the effort.

If you could meet your future self, what advice do you think you would give your current self? Picture yourself ten, twenty, and fifty years from now. What do you envision having accomplished? Begin NOW setting daily steps for those things to come true. Your next-week/next-month/next-year future self isn't going to be any more motivated to take those steps than you are right now today. It's the small daily steps that get you to your goal.

Making the difference only you can make

My friend, Isaac, ran into a burning building to save a baby. Really. It's the kind of thing they make movies about. At three a.m. one night, a fire alarm blared, awakening Isaac and his friend. Stumbling out of their apartment, they heard the cries of a young mother who couldn't reach her baby before the flames drove her out of her own burning apartment. As soon as Isaac realized what was happening, he ran into the burning apartment and got the baby out safely.

> **If I am afraid, lazy, or unmotivated, wanting to binge a season on Netflix instead of working hard to reach my potential, what then? No one will be motivated by my silent voice or my unwritten work.**

Given this gift of life, being snatched from the flames, I wonder what will become of this child. Will he grow up knowing that he barely escaped death? Will he be careful to live to his full potential, knowing that someone else valued his life so highly that he risked his own to save it?

It's easy to draw the parallels of Isaac's action to our own. Although you may not be running into burning buildings literally saving lives, what if you are the one who should write something or say something that will encourage someone else to live to their fullest potential?

If Isaac had not run into the building, would the baby have been saved? What if Isaac had been too afraid, or unmotivated, or had decided to wait on the professionals who were still a full five minutes away? (I'm not advocating running into burning buildings, by the way! This was a once-in-a-lifetime hero moment for Isaac.)

If I am afraid, lazy, or unmotivated, wanting to binge a season on Netflix instead of working hard to reach my potential, what then? Although not as dramatic as Isaac's heroic effort, I am still responsible to the world. No one will be motivated by my silent voice or my unwritten work.

Take your talents and your gifts and especially those things that you are good at and enjoy and develop them fully. Make it your life's goal to work hard to become the best version of yourself. Set high standards and challenge yourself to meet them.

> *Adulting Like a Boss means knowing what it takes to be an adult and to do it fearlessly. Adulting is hard but it's a learning process and it takes time.*
>
> *Lulay H – 25*

Choose to always be moving ahead

We all have the opportunity to choose the path we take in life. Though some circumstances may inhibit how many choices you may have, everyone has a choice of attitude. While it may not be true of every person on earth, most of us have unlimited choices in what careers we choose, what relationships we pursue (or don't pursue), and how we respond to the difficulties life throws at us.

When you are young, you say what you want to be when you grow up.

> *I want to be a doctor.*
> *I want to be a flight attendant.*
> *I want to be a mom.*

Amazingly, you can choose your life. You can literally write your own story. Study hard and opportunities for education will present themselves. Work hard and advancement will come.

You get to choose. If part of your story is already written, you can choose the next chapter.

Do you remember the *Choose Your Own Adventure* books? At the end of each chapter, you would be given the choice – *Does Susan go into the cave? Turn to page 79. Does Susan wait for her friend to arrive? Turn to page 122.* (Not this book, silly. In the *Choose Your Own Adventure* book.)

That's your life. Choose. Choose what's next.

As you move ahead in life, choose the following qualities to Adult Like a Boss:
- Choose to be happy.
- Choose to always be moving ahead.
- Choose kindness.
- Choose to finish what you start.
- Choose patience.

Not tomorrow. Not next week or next month or next year. NOW is your time.

Do an act of kindness when you're sure
no one will find out it was you.

— Laura Thomae Young

– 5 –

ADULTING WITH POSITIVITY

"Keep striving to become the absolute best version of yourself, surrounding yourself with love and lovely people, embracing life with both hands, and filling your life to overflow with wonder, amazement, and joy."

Do you know the story of a bucket of crabs?

When you go crabbing, that is, catching crabs in the wild for a crab boil, you grab one and throw it into a bucket. Pretty soon you'll have a bucket full of crabs piled so high that the ones on top of the pile can climb out. But any crab who begins to climb out of the bucket is *pulled back down* by the others. They don't want anyone to escape!

> **Friends who are down often sabotage those who aspire to do better. They will pull you down with their negative comments, discouragement, and sometimes even attempt to make you feel guilty for your success.**

Much like those crazy crabs, friends who are down often sabotage those who aspire to do better. They will pull you down with their negative comments, discouragement, and sometimes even attempt to make you feel guilty for your success. In all of your relationships, look for people who are going to lift you up, not pull you down! Look for relationships where you feel you *must* be your best to keep up.

Surround yourself with friends who are going places in their careers, life goals, and relationships. You may have to branch out to find them – yes, outside of your comfort zone! Find them! Where do they hang out? What activities are they participating in? Go THERE. Do THAT! Do the Hard Thing!

Surround yourself with motivating people

I hang out with people I'm not quite sure I'm good enough or smart enough or cool enough to hang out with because they make me push myself. If I want to be more active, hanging out with lazy friends is never going to push me. If I want to eat right, then hanging out with my friends at the fast food restaurant is not going to cut it. I push myself, but I have to stay motivated. And there's nothing better than being around highly energetic and motivated people.

Adulting with Positivity

If it's true that you are the sum of the five people you spend the most time with, then I am careful about who those five people are! I want to be creative and push myself creatively, so I choose to spend my time with musicians and writers and podcasters and bloggers. My daughter is studying medicine, so she surrounds herself with folks who are equally driven to study and make good grades.

Surrounding yourself with people who are living uninspired lives will never push you into greatness. It will, instead, draw you into contentedness with mediocre living.

Have a positive attitude

Did you know that you can choose your attitude – even through tough times? Don't believe me? Let me give you an example.

In a corporate office where I worked, there were two co-workers whose jobs were to speak with (mostly elderly) customers on the phone. The co-workers were kind and compassionate, speaking gently with the customers as they explained our company's service to them.

However, the two co-workers didn't get along. They were sour, rude even, and never had a nice tone when speaking with one another.

> **Attitude follows behavior. Treat others respectfully and you'll soon find yourself respecting them.**

It amazed me that in one second they could change from a kind and compassion tone with the customer to a snarl with each other. It was a choice. Their behavior reflected their attitudes.

Oftentimes, though, attitude follows the behavior. Speak kindly to someone you don't particularly like, and you'll find that a kind attitude begins to develop. Treat others respectfully and you'll soon find yourself respecting them.

You can *choose* to be positive and happy regardless of your surroundings. Looking at the glass half-full is a challenge when life's circumstances are difficult. It doesn't mean that you don't accept sorrow or pain as an inevitable part of life. What it does mean, though, is that the practice of choosing a positive attitude can change the way you view those circumstances. Here are a couple of ways you can put that into practice:

> **If negative self-talk diminishes your self-worth — and it definitely does — then positive self-talk will build you up.**

- **Positivity** – Being predictably positive and affirmative about yourself and your work - as well as being an encouragement to others will do more for you in your career and your life than another class, course, or degree. Everyone likes to be around positive and encouraging people, and, frankly, nobody wants to be around someone who complains, whines, and belittles themselves or others.

- **Positive People** – As already mentioned, surround yourself with positive people. One of the best ways you can help yourself is to surround yourself with others who are positive and moving ahead in their lives. If you surround yourself with those who are negative, down in the dumps, "Why me?" and aren't moving forward in their lives, you will likely get pulled down with them.

Watch your words

Do you find yourself saying things about yourself that you would never say about someone else? Things like, "I can't" and "I never" and other self-sabotaging words? Words have power. When your ears hear your own words spoken out loud, that message bounces right into your brain and into your heart.

> **Using positive words throughout the day helps to pick up your mood and attitude.**

In contrast, positive, affirming self-talk really works. Tell yourself OUT LOUD that you are amazing. Cite your best qualities and use a power pose! Say it aloud in a confident voice. It may feel silly when you first start doing it, but if negative self-talk diminishes your self-worth – and it definitely does – then positive self-talk will build you up.

Enlace positive words into your vocabulary. Try saying "fantastic" with a frowny face. It can't be done! Using positive words throughout the day helps to pick up your mood and attitude. Fantastic might not be *your* word, but find what that positive word is for you and use it often. Use it to describe your day as well as how you feel about who you are and what you are doing.

How's that project going, Amy? FANTASTIC!
How are you feeling today, Bethany? GREAT!
You may not feel fantastic or great. But using positive words in a believable tone will head you in that direction.

Serve others

When I was a little girl, my mother would pack all of us kids into the car and drive down to the local old folks' home to visit the elderly residents. Sometimes we would sing for them, passing out kiddie band instruments for the residents to play along with the music. We'd shake every hand, pass out candies, and make sure that every person knew how special they were.

There were some folks there who had regular visits from family and friends, but always there were others who had no one. It was a joy to us to bring a little ray of sunshine into an otherwise bleak existence.

Rinse and repeat and I have taken my own children many times to the nursing homes and senior centers to do the same thing. There is much to be gained in your character by serving others in a humble way.

Doing something for others, with no expectation of reciprocation, is good for the soul.

Look for ways to serve your community. Volunteer.

In Nashville, where I live, there is an organization that puts together a list of all the places that need volunteers. If you have a day, a week, or a month, they'll match your skill set with a group or organization where you can serve. From painting a school to planting a community garden, there's something for everyone.

You may not have the advantage of everything being so clear-cut and tailor-made for you, so finding the right fit may take a little more effort. It might be hard. Do the Hard Thing and find out what's available.

> **Doing something for others, with no expectation of reciprocation, is good for the soul.**

It's not enough just to find out all about it, though. Call around and find out what's available and when, then make a commitment. Tell the person, I'll be there on *this* day and here's how many hours I will volunteer.

Most volunteers will tell you that they personally benefit from the work they do far more than the organization does. The intrinsic value of volunteering is great. Knowing that you are helping your fellow man and knowing that you are doing something good with your time is worth any hassle it will be to get there and do the job.

When you think of volunteering for a nonprofit, things like community gardens, painting a school, or other physical projects are what typically come to mind, but there are many other types of volunteer projects, like visiting a nursing home or hospital, making baskets or boxes for gifts to the needy or sick, typing up a flyer, passing out programs at a community theater, or doing the social media push an organization needs for fundraising. There are all kinds of opportunities, so check around. Look for nonprofits, churches, civic organizations, political groups, or other community organizations.

You do volunteer work because it's good to be involved in the community, but DO keep a written journal of what you're doing, when you're doing it, and how many hours you're putting in. I worked for a company who wanted to keep a log of their employees' volunteer hours. This allowed them to give a shout out to the community about their contributions.

You may also want to add your volunteer service to your resume the next time you are applying for a job. I've looked at zillions of resumes for potential employees, and volunteering, added at the bottom of the resume, often catches my eye.

Be sure and check out the *"How To"* on volunteering on the next page.

Keep striving to become the absolute best version of yourself, surrounding yourself with love and lovely people, embracing life with both hands, and filling your life to overflow with wonder, amazement, and joy.

HOW TO...

Volunteer Like a Boss!

- **Ask if you need to bring anything with you** – Tools? Gloves? Food? Make a list of whatever they tell you and purchase or borrow it. Consider donating any items you purchase for that day's work unless you plan to return and will need the item again (a shovel, work gloves, or other items you may not normally use).
- **Put it on your schedule** – Volunteering, like any other activity outside of the "musts" that are on your list, is going to take some commitment. It's unlikely that there will be a day when you are wondering what in the world to do, and you decide to volunteer. Making a commitment to a certain day or week may be inconvenient or difficult. That's normal. People who spend time volunteering often aren't doing it because they don't have other commitments and things to do. Rather, they prioritize their volunteer activities above other things. Saying yes to volunteering will mean saying no to other activities.
- **Set a reminder** – Once you've made the commitment, put it on your calendar so that you don't forget. Those who run volunteer groups are used to people flaking out at the last minute, and you don't want to be that person. If you are supposed to bring anything with you, such as tools or toys or food, you'll want to mark that on your calendar a day or so before, so you don't use being ill-prepared as an excuse not to go.
- **Enlist a friend to go with you** – Find someone to do it with you and you'll be much more likely to follow through. Plus it may make it even more enjoyable to have someone with you.
- **Be sure to show up** – Most nonprofits need volunteers and will be counting on your help. Make sure you show up and work hard. Arrive early and stay later than planned.

- **Carve out the time** – Perhaps you don't have time in your schedule (though I encourage you to make the time) to volunteer regularly. In that case, decide on a time frame, and carve out the time to volunteer. One day a month? One week a year? It's for you to decide, but you should be giving back to your community and world by volunteering.

Your dream job may be down the road a bit.
Do the hard stuff now, learning and growing
to be ready to take the dream job.

— Laura Thomae Young

– 6 –

ADULTING THROUGH MEANINGFUL WORK

*"To find meaningful work and to do it with all your heart will give you a great feeling of satisfaction. It is the freedom that was longed for, but not found, in the sixties rebellion.
It is freedom through responsibility!"*

In the 2000 film *Castaway*, Tom Hanks's character is trapped on a deserted island. After days of surviving on coconuts and raw fish, he finally figures out how to create fire. He makes a huge bonfire on the beach and dances around it, shouting, "Look at me! I have created FIRE!" His award-winning performance draws you into the enormous feeling of satisfaction that he had conquered the task of making fire.

Adulting Like a Boss

If you've ever created a work of art, painted a room, or even cleaned out a closet, you know the satisfaction of standing back and admiring a job well done. It's a feeling of accomplishment and pride.

We live in a world of constant entertainment choices. Television, internet, video games, movies, theater, sporting events, even news media - they are all used to entertain. Until the past few decades, entertainment was a reward for a hard day or week of work. Today entertainment is constant, and we only tolerate our life's work. It doesn't have to – and shouldn't – be that way. Be ever so careful that entertainment does not become your chief end. Entertainment has its rightful place in your life, but meaningful work is what will give your life satisfaction and meaning.

Our American society, for the past hundred years, has created an opportunity that is unprecedented throughout history. The opportunity is that you get to choose your own career path. Since pretty much forever, people have been conscripted, assigned, or born into a career path. It was unlikely that they would stray far from their family's footprints in their career. In contrast, today it is not at all expected that you will follow in your father or mother's footprints. From the time you are small, people begin asking you, "What do you want to be when you grow up?" You get to choose.

> Not "What am I told to contribute?," or "What do I want to contribute?," but the question should be, "What *should* I contribute?"

Historically, if your father or mother were in a career, then society's expectations were that you would follow right along. Children were not free to explore their talents and gifts and go their own way. Often they began apprenticing underneath their parents to become a partner and eventually take over the family business. Farmers begat more farmers. Blacksmiths begat blacksmiths. Midwives trained their daughters to deliver and care for babies.

This is the way it was, but in most modern societies, this is no longer the expectation. Of course it does still sometimes happen. Farmers often do train their kids who eventually take over the family farm business. Doctors and lawyers many times have their sons and daughters practicing in partnerships with the parents. But for the most part, it is because of choice, not conscription or even expectation. Nowadays people will say to a doctor whose son or daughter also goes into medicine, "How delighted you must be to have Billy or Suzy working beside you." It's not expected, but cool when it happens.

> Your career choice should be aligned with your personal values. If not, you'll feel sleazy trying to work for a company that contributes something to the world that you do not believe is right.

A well-known management consultant, educator and author, Peter Drucker (1909-2005) wrote about this in a chapter of his book *Management Challenges for the 21st Century*. The chapter, "Managing Oneself" has been reprinted a number of times. In the chapter, he attributes the shift in thinking to the changes that occurred in the sixties, when rebellion against society's expectations occurred and more people were free to "do their own thing." But according to Drucker, the license that was taken didn't lead to fulfillment or success.

> *To me, Adulting Like a Boss means accepting that I will never have it "all together." When I graduated, I felt ready to conquer the world. I learned some of my hardest and most memorable lessons when I realized that I was ONLY 22 and (because I don't do open heart surgery) my job was never THAT serious. Once I finally allowed myself to be content with my mistakes, it made room for people with experience to help me because they were once in my shoes. Adulting Like a Boss is letting my inner voice confidently tell me, "Oops – I totally screwed up here. But, it's cool. I got this."*
>
> --Vannesia D., 27

Drucker says that the question we should ask ourselves is not "What am I *told* to contribute?" as it was in the days of following in your parents' occupational footsteps, nor "What do I *want* to contribute?" as it was in the sixties. Rather, Drucker states, and I agree, the question should be, "What *should* I contribute?"

If we base our career (and/or side hustle, if you're not feeling you've chosen the right career path) on our strengths and desires, then the "should" won't be burdensome, but fulfilling. Our contribution to the world will be gratifying. It's when we work in opposition to our gifts that our career feels arduous.

Working within your strengths, your career choice

and the company you choose to spend your days working for should be aligned with your personal values. If not, you'll feel sleazy trying to work for a company that contributes something to the world that you do not believe is right.

Now here's the thing: You can't necessarily determine all of this in the first days, weeks, or months of a new career. Especially if you are gifted in many areas and hold multiple talents and interests, you may have a harder time determining what your contribution to the world *should* be. Simon Sinek's video "Millennials in the Workplace" affirms the same belief. It takes time.

In the age of instant everything, there are still some things that take time. This is one of them. Unless you are doing something you really hate or your job is utterly detestable to your values, stick with it for at least a year. Learn everything you can, grow however you can, and at the end of a good strong year of attempting to be the star employee, reevaluate. Even if you're feeling unfulfilled or that you're not making a mark on the world, stick with it for a time. You have much to learn, and though you may have your eye on the summit, as Simon Sinek states, you still have the mountain before you.

> **Learn everything you can [in your job], grow however you can, and at the end of a good strong year of attempting to be the star employee, reevaluate.**

There is nothing – I repeat – *nothing* more internally rewarding than a job well done. To find meaningful work and to do it with all your heart will give you a great feeling of satisfaction. It is the freedom that was longed for, but not found, in the sixties rebellion. It is freedom through responsibility.

Responsibility doesn't sound fun or sexy, but it is responsibility that makes the world go 'round. Taking responsibility for your work makes you Adult Like a Boss.

Time spent with family and friends
is time well spent.

— Laura Thomae Young

– 7 –

ADULTING WITH YOUR DECISIONS

*"Decision-making is like a muscle –
the more it is exercised, the stronger it gets."*

Adulting Like a Boss means making decisions and following through with them.

Why is it so hard to make a decision? The truth is, we all make decisions every day – from the little ones – what you're going to eat for dinner, what to wear to work, whether or not you're going to work out – to the big ones – where you're going to live, who you're going to enter into a relationship with, and what career path to take.

There are lots of reasons we might put off making a decision, but the root cause is usually fear. We are afraid of making the wrong decision, especially the big decisions that have big consequences. So, we paralyze ourselves and make no decision. But NOT deciding is also a decision. Not deciding is saying, "NO" for now.

There have been several occasions in my life where stalling a decision caused me to miss out on an opportunity. Most recently, this occurred with buying a house. The housing market is booming where we live, and if you hesitate making an offer, the house will be gone before you even get a chance. After looking at several houses in a neighborhood we liked, we found two that we loved. I couldn't decide between House A and House B. The reality was, either house was absolutely perfect. Because there were pros and cons to both, I kept weighing the decision – back and forth. Once I finally decided on House A, it was too late.

> **NOT deciding is also a decision. Not deciding is saying, "NO" for now.**

After the disappointment of seeing House A slip through my fingers, I was afraid I would be settling for the second choice by making an offer on House B. And I hesitated again. Finally, my realtor, who was also a friend, called me and asked me what I was waiting for. He knew stalling any longer would make us lose the opportunity for House B too. Thankfully, his encouragement to make a decision was just the push I needed, and we made an offer. We've been happily enjoying House B for several years. Once I made that hard decision and moved forward, I was relieved. I've never felt like it was second best.

When you procrastinate making a decision, you are putting your life on hold and letting opportunities slip by. Making a decision is the first step to ACTION. Without making a decision, you won't take that first step. To reach any goal – small or large, you have to take that first step. You're guaranteed to *never* reach your goal if you don't take that first step.

The benefits you'll get from making decisions

Here are a few benefits you'll gain by being a decision-maker:

- **Less stress**: If you're stressed out by decisions, you'll find that once the decision is made, you don't have to spend time worrying about it anymore.

- **More time**: Once the decision is made, you'll find you can accomplish more. You're not spending countless precious moments procrastinating, but instead, you'll be moving ahead toward your goals.

> You're guaranteed to never reach your goal if you don't take that first step.

- **Leadership opportunities**: Those who make decisions and make them quickly will find that others will want to follow them. If you want to be a leader with a team of people behind you who can accomplish more than you can accomplish by yourself, then learn to make decisions.

If you're the kind of person who goes back and forth, can't make up your mind, puts off the decision until the last minute, or worse, doesn't make one at all, I have encouragement for you! YOU CAN CHANGE.

Decision-making is like a muscle - the more it is exercised, the stronger it gets. Studies have shown that we are better at making decisions (a)

> *I knew I was really grown up when I got a promotion at work. I became a supervisor, and I was 23 at the time. On the one hand, I thought I was really young and fresh out of college and still trying to figure stuff out, and on the other hand, I had to supervise people. So, I just had to put my big-girl pants on and do what I had to, in order to be successful in my new role.*
> *--Duaa A – 24*

earlier in the day, (b) when we're not hungry, and (c) when we aren't fatigued from making too many decisions.

If you have an important decision to make, choose a time to weigh it out when you are well rested, it is early in the day, and you have eaten a good meal. You'll find that you have much more clarity. Then, stick with the choice you make. Follow it through to the end. Don't go back and forth.

There are only a few life decisions that are irreversible, and ninety-nine percent of the decisions we pull our hair out over are not in that category.

Systems, rituals, habits – these all serve to prevent you from having to make a million little decisions and allow space to make the big ones.

How to make a good decision

If you have a big life decision to make, use the following four steps to make the process easier:

1. **Do the recon** – Gather all the facts you can find on the subject. Research, dig, read. Ask other people about their experience in a similar situation. Ask for their opinion. You aren't asking anyone to tell you what to do; you're simply gathering information. Ask people not only the "what," but also *why* they feel the way they do.

2. **Weigh it out** – Once you've gathered information, make a pros and cons list. Think about consequences or long-term outcomes. Think about the unchangeability of the decision.

3. **Picture yourself** – In a few weeks or months, which scenario seems more favorable? Picture yourself telling your best friend why you chose *this* or *that* decision. Which feels more right?

4. **Make the decision and don't look back** – Once it's made, stop thinking about alternatives. Done. Decided. Now move on.

> **There are only a few life decisions that are irreversible, and 99% of the decisions we pull our hair out over are not in that category.**

Now that you've made the big decision, stick with it, at least for a time. Don't think it didn't work because you're tired of trying and it's hard. Remember that Adulting is doing the *Hard* Thing. Give yourself a specific date or time to reevaluate your decision, and until that date, *be all in*. One-hundred percent committed to the decision you have made. Yeah, now you're Adulting Like a Boss!

It's hard. Do it anyway.

— Laura Thomae Young

– 8 –

ADULTING MEANS TAKING CARE OF YOURSELF

"The negative consequences from sloppy habits and harmful behavior are coming. It may be weeks, months, or years down the road, but ultimately, you'll reap what you sow."

The one person who cares the most about you is... YOU!

Your mom might be a close second, but ultimately, *you* are your own best advocate for getting your life together, for learning something new, balancing your bank account, making a doctor's appointment, getting promoted, eating right and exercising, and, generally, *doing the Hard Thing*.

Adulting Like a Boss

When you're in school, there's pressure and structure and extrinsic forces at work – your parents, your teachers and professors, deadlines, and grades. Once you're out on your own, the force to be reckoned with has to be *you*.

> **Ultimately, you are your own best advocate for getting your life together.**

If there's a promotion or another job that would be perfect for you, it's unlikely that anyone is going to come ask you to take it. Nobody is going to tell you to update your resume. Nobody is going to hit the "send" button on the email. It has to be *you*.

And that's where the *Hard Thing* comes in. You have to advocate and care for yourself, because nobody is going to do it for you. And nobody is going to tell you to do it.

Here's the thing though - *you* are amazing! YOU take care of yourself. YOU choose to eat right, and take care of your things, and put yourself out there. YOU can do it.

Step up and let your boss know you are perfect for the promotion. Call the doctor and make the appointment. Plan your meals and do the shopping for healthy food and stick to it. Be the number-one fan of YOU.

Adulting Like a Boss means taking care of yourself, your belongings, your money, your time, and your relationships. It's doing the Hard Thing when the easy thing is…well, easier. It's looking down the road and seeing the long-term good from doing the Hard Thing now and the long-term negative consequences that come with doing the easy thing.

The Opposite of Delayed Gratification = Delayed Consequences.
If you don't eat right, nothing happens right away that you can see. It's often months or years before you reap those negative benefits. So, you stay up late at night eating pizza and drinking too much wine, then get up the next morning and eat donuts – and what happens? Nothing. So if nothing bad happens, it must be okay. You do it again and again, and nobody tells you not to, because you're right there with your friends who are doing it too. There's no parent or teacher or doctor that is going to call you up and scold you. And a thickening waist line... well that may not happen until you're thirty. And heart problems from eating like that? Ah, those are years away, right?

Delayed consequences are a bugger, because we tell ourselves quiet little lies.

- "If there are no consequences NOW then there are no consequences at all."
- "I'm exempt from consequences that other people reap."
- "This behavior is temporary. I'll change it 'later.' When I'm an adult."

> Once you're out on your own, the force to be reckoned with has to be you.

It's time to start the Hard Thing. Do the right thing, and do it now. The negative consequences from sloppy habits and harmful behavior are coming. It may be weeks, months, or years down the road, but ultimately, you'll reap what you sow.

Conversely, the opposite is also true. You'll reap *good* things when you take care of your body, your relationships, your job, and yourself.

I knew I was really grown up when I first began to acknowledge that I am in fact a human being who has valid physical needs (sleep, food, and affection), not a self-sacrificing robot that can do everything for everyone at all times. There's a part of me that still wants to believe that taking care of my needs is selfish, but thankfully I have a lot of empirical proof saying otherwise: I'm most able to take care of the people I love when I am attentive to my limits. When I was just ignoring needs and trying to make them go away, I was actually more standoffish and afraid to engage with new people, and less generous with my closest friends. It's still tough acknowledging those needs sometimes, because I like to think that I'm actually a superhero, but I'm not, and no one literally is, and that is really okay.

--Emily E., 25

Eat right and exercise, and you'll have a healthy body. Have a regular sleep pattern and you'll feel rested and energetic. Pick up after yourself and you'll have a tidy space to live in.

Take care of you.
Advocate for you.
Love you.

Self-indulgence is not self-love.

Suppose you have a friend with a toddler. You're sitting together on the park bench watching her little darling play in the park. She confides in you her philosophy of child-rearing.

"I'm going to give him absolutely everything

he desires any time he requests it," she says. "I'm going to do whatever it takes to make sure he is never denied anything. He's going to get what he wants, when he wants it. That's love. That will make him happy."

You would probably stare at her in shock. Everybody knows that this kind of indulgence will lead to a spoiled, bratty kid, *and* it can be dangerous or unhealthy. Let's say the kid wants to only eat candy and never eat vegetables. Maybe he wants to play in the street and not the park. Of course he doesn't want to share his toys with his sister. You see where this is going?

That's not love. That's indulgence.

That won't lead to happiness. That will likely lead to UN-happiness. For both the mother and the child.

Yet for some reason, we treat ourselves like the friend treats her child.

We want to do something, and we do it without thinking of the consequences. We don't deny ourselves. We don't discipline ourselves.

Fast food versus healthy food. Television versus reading. A weekend lying on the couch binge watching dramatic television versus community volunteering. A shopping trip for things we don't need versus a savings account. Laziness versus sports or exercise.

Now I don't mean to say that we should never treat ourselves. Going back to the example of your friend's child, she may sometimes give him a piece of candy as a treat. (Yes, I know there are lots of people who would never use candy as a treat, that it can lead to all kinds of wrong ideas about the relationship with food, years of therapy, etc., but just go with me here.)

> **It's doing the hard thing when the easy thing is...well, easier.**

A treat is an occasional indulgence. Something out of the ordinary that happens only once in a while. They're fun. They're rewards to ourselves for doing the Hard Things. But a life of all treats – all candy and no vegetables – leads to a life of rotting teeth and flabby bodies.

"Deny yourself" is not a popular theme. "Discipline yourself" doesn't make it to the front cover of the pop magazines.

The headlines that make it to the front are:

- "Eat everything you want AND use this little gizmo, and you'll lose weight."
- "You deserve it all."
- "Buy this thing, because you deserve it."

Thus, we've equated indulgence with self-love.

But what if the opposite is true?

What if self-love is doing the Hard Thing?

What if, in order to lose weight, for example, you *can't* have everything you want, and it *is* hard work to eat right and exercise? What if it takes an enormous amount of effort to plan menus, grocery shop, cook, and make trips to the gym?

Adulting Means Taking Care of Yourself

What if, to reach your big awesome goals, it's not as easy as three quick steps? What if it takes, instead, years of excruciatingly hard work, early mornings and late nights, missing out on your favorite show?

What if relationships are hard and messy, and you screw them up sometimes, but you keep pushing through and finally get to a place where the two of you have a groove and truly enjoy one another? But what if it takes years of ups and downs to get there?

What if you have to work extremely hard at a job you don't really like for a couple years before you can find the fulfillment you were hoping to get out of your career? Or work two side jobs so you can support yourself while you pursue your dream?

> "Deny yourself" is not a popular theme. "Discipline yourself" doesn't make it to the front cover of the pop magazines. Self-denial and discipline — they're not sexy, but they're essential.

What if you have to do the Hard Thing – and do it a lot – to finally get the good stuff in life?

Self-denial and discipline – they're not sexy, but they're essential.

Turn off the television and
go outside and play.

— My mom

– 9 –

ADULTING WITH YOUR HEALTH

"If you don't take care of your body... where are you gonna' live?"

If you are in your first office job out of college, it's likely a big shock to your body!

Back at school, you were probably used to walking from class to class, to the library, to your apartment, up and down stairs, down long hallways. Sit down, stand up, in and out. In college, you're more likely to participate in lots of activities outside of class that keep you active – sports, walking or jogging, fun group activities in and outside of school.

You'll find the corporate environment to be quite different.

Adulting Like a Boss

Imagine this scenario – because it's been mine before. To get to work each morning, you walk out to your car – just a few steps away from your front door. You drive to work and park. The office door is just a few steps away.

You take your seat at your cubicle, and except for a short mid-morning break, you sit. And sit. And sit.

> **Congratulations! You completed *three-hundred* steps today on your FitBit!**

Lunch is whatever you brought from home or whatever you can grab – thirty to sixty minutes, if you're lucky - and sometimes you even eat it at your desk. (By the way – that's not a good idea!)

Now you return from lunch, sit down at your desk where you remain for the afternoon, and voila, it's five o'clock! You walk the few steps back to your car. Drive home, walk from your car to your apartment, plop down on the couch for the evening, eat leftover Chinese food from the day before, and binge watch television shows until you fall asleep.

You completed three-hundred steps today on your FitBit.

Monday through Friday, that's the routine. Day after day of this will kill you! But this is how many people live.

Going from college to corporate is a big life change. You won't have all of the ready-made activities that keep you moving and fit. You have to be very deliberate to *stay moving*. You will need to make daily decisions to add steps and keep from becoming a sedentary potato!

Now, let's imagine a very different scenario:

Adulting with Your Health

You wake up early, I mean *really* early. You're rested because last night you chose to go to bed a little earlier than usual, foregoing the Netflix binge. It's still dark outside, but that's okay, because you are **POWER**. You are **AMAZE**. You are **CONQUER**.

You brush your teeth, splash water on your face, and fix a cup of hot brew. And now you sit - erect, power pose - and you meditate on your upcoming day. You breathe. You pray. You think deeply. You speak aloud and affirm your dreams and actions for the day. You visualize yourself having already achieved your goals. You count your blessings. You are thankful. You are fully alive.

Now it's time to get outside. The sun is beginning to come out, and you are already dressed in your exercise clothes. A quick jog, listening to your favorite tunes, and you return home invigorated and ready for the day. Shower, dress for work, and jump in the car.

> **Investing in your body at a young age will help you now and when you are older.**

You park at the end of the lot so you'll get in your extra steps. You choose the stairs instead of the elevator. You power-walk on a break as you make a quick call to Mom to say hello (see how I slipped that in there?). Back at work you stand often, stretch, and walk on your break after eating a healthy lunch you packed yourself.

Now it's five o'clock and you head home. You change clothes and get out to the park to play a game of softball on the community team. Or head to the gym. Or meet a friend for dinner. Or take in the community theater's latest production.

Exercise

Be deliberate about getting out and exercising. To be consistent, you'll need to make it fun. Join a gym and work out with a friend. Join an exercise class. Meet up with a walking or jogging partner. Participate in community sports activities.

The good thing about all of those is that it doesn't matter if you're a professional athlete or a newbie at sports - community leagues don't care. Just go and have fun. You'll learn! And this will serve as both exercise AND meeting people!

Eating right and exercising is, of course, important for your current health. But they are also critical for your *future* health. Weight-bearing exercise builds strong bones and helps prevent osteoporosis in your later years, (that's the condition of weakened bones that causes older women to be hunched over *and* to easily break bones). So, investing in your body at a young age will help you now *and* when you are older.

Creating healthy habits and an active lifestyle of good foods and lots of movement *now* will help you keep those habits throughout your life. You're not going to suddenly wake up when you're forty years old and feel like starting. You're less likely to start later in life when the pounds really love your hips, so do it *now*. Do the Hard Thing (creating habits of exercise) now so you get the EASY thing (health) later.

When given the choice, choose to DO. When presented with the option, choose to MOVE. Be fully alive and treat your body as a temple. Use every ounce of energy every day – don't worry, you'll get more tomorrow!

(I'm singing in my head, "I Like to Move it Move it!")

Doctor and Dentist

So…the doctor and the dentist. Making your own appointments, signing yourself in, filling out your own paperwork, knowing your health history (and that of your family) – that's the real deal in Adulting!

First of all - yep, you gotta go! If you're sick and you need to go to the doctor, you're going to have to do this thing. And you should be making regular visits to the "lady doctor" because you're a girl and that's what you're supposed to do. (If you're a guy reading this book, you can ignore that last sentence.)

Why you need to find a doctor.

When you're sick or not feeling well, you don't want the added stress of going to a new place, meeting a new doctor, and having to write out a complete history of

> Sometime when you're not sick and you have a few minutes, take some time to find a doctor.

everything that everyone in your family has ever had! You just want to get in, get diagnosed, get some meds and get back home. It's so much better to have already established a relationship with a primary care doctor before you're actually sick. When you're coughing up a lung or doubled over in pain, the last thing in the world you feel like doing is meeting someone new.

> **Use every ounce of energy every day — don't worry, you'll get more tomorrow!**

And don't worry if your doctor isn't really a "doctor." Most clinics have Physician Assistants (PA) and Nurse Practitioners (NP), who diagnose, treat, and write prescriptions just like a doctor can.

Many primary care doctors will offer a "get-to-know-you" visit to establish the doctor-patient relationship. Check your insurance policy to see what kinds of visits are covered. Often there will be a general checkup that is covered at 100%.

If you're sick, go to the doctor. A doctor's office may not be your favorite place to hang out, but it is a much better option than a 2:00 a.m. visit to the emergency room.

The gyno (Again, if you're a dude, you can skip this part.)

A gynecologist visit is an important part of a woman's health. A gynecologist is a doctor who specializes in fertility, birth control, cancer prevention, sexually transmitted diseases, and other women's health issues.

Every woman should get routine Pap smears (testing for cancer, pre-cancer, and other cell abnormalities) and breast exams by a doctor, and you should learn to do breast self-exams correctly. My breast-cancer-survivor friend, who is also a nurse, won't let me forget this, as she had noticed a lump in her own routine self-exam. She's now a seven-year survivor.

How often you should go for regular checkups is under some debate, and I defer you to your personal doctor. If you have an abnormal Pap, your doctor will want to see you more often. If everything is normal, most doctors will ask you to come back in a couple of years.

If you want to begin or continue using birth control, like IUD, birth control pills, or other options, a gynecologist office is a good place to establish a relationship. There are clinics that specialize only in birth control, but since you have to go somewhere, go ahead and get to know a doctor who can do more comprehensive women's health care.

If you're thinking of having children sometime in the future, you will want to make sure your gynecologist also practices obstetrics (aka, delivering babies). If you feel strongly about home births, using a midwife, or other similar options, ask about those things before you begin going to a new doctor. Some doctors are open to those options, but others may not be as favorable toward them.

> **Many primary care doctors will offer a "get-to-know-you" visit to establish the doctor-patient relationship.**

How do I find a doctor?

Sometime when you're *not* sick and you have a few minutes, take some time to find a doctor. Here are a few steps and tips for getting started:

- **Ask friends and family who live in the area for recommendations.** For general care you'll want a family doctor or an internist, who will serve as your Primary Care Physician (PCP). They'll take care of things like viruses, flu, sinus infections, urinary tract infections, and other common problems.

If you need a specialist, or have something more serious going on, you'll likely also need a referral, which you'll get from your PCP.

- **Conduct a search on your health-care provider's website.** If you have health insurance, log on to your provider's website and do a search. You can search by specialty, proximity to your home, the doctor's gender, and other filters. If you already have a doctor in mind, check if he or she is on the provider's website - you'll most likely want to go to a doctor who accepts your insurance, otherwise known as an In-Network doctor. Most insurance policies require you to pay more for Out-of-Network doctors, (who don't actually accept your insurance). You can still go to them, but it will cost you much more than it would to visit an In-Network doctor, and you'll have to file the insurance claim yourself.

- **Make sure the doctor is accepting new patients.** Most clinics have a maximum census of patients they can handle, and once they're full, they can't accept new patients until some of their census members drop off. Even if the insurance website *says* they accept your insurance and take new patients, call and ask first. I've found that the info on the website is often outdated.

- **Get a general checkup.** If you haven't had one in a while, make an appointment for a general checkup. If you have recently had one but you need to find a new doctor, see if you can make a general appointment to establish a relationship with a new primary care doctor.

What about a dentist?

- I recommend that you have dental insurance if your employer provides it. Costs through your employer usually range between $20-$30 per month, and buying dental insurance privately can be about the same.

- If you have dental insurance, check online and see which dentists in your area accept your insurance. And again, ask family, friends, or co-workers for recommendations.

- Almost all dental plans will pay 100% for two preventative check-ups and cleanings a year, including x-rays. Most plans then cover a portion of dental work. Check your policy.

- Take advantage of the twice-a-year visits. Any dental problems should be taken care of right away, because they'll only get worse. This is a big ol' Adulting thing to do, one you won't regret!

- If you don't have dental insurance, consider going to a dental school to get your dental work done. At a dental school, advanced students do the work under the supervision of the dentists who are teaching them. Several of my family and friends have received excellent dental care for a fraction of the cost of a regular dentist.

> **Even if the insurance website says they accept your insurance and take new patients, call and ask first. I've found that the info on the website is often outdated.**

If you don't find a good fit – you don't like the doctor or dentist you've chosen or you don't think they treated you well - go ahead and look elsewhere. There might be another doctor in the same clinic that would be a better fit. Be patient (no pun intended), and take your time until you find someone you connect with and can respect. Having a doctor you like will make you more willing to go when you need to.

Do the Hard Thing here! Make yourself do it! Nobody WANTS to go to the doctor or dentist (well, almost nobody), but it's an important Adult thing to do to take care of yourself.

If you don't take care of your body…where are you gonna' live?

HOW TO...

Host a Party at Home that Everyone Talks About for Weeks

Hosting a party at your own place can be lots of fun, but it can also be stressful if you're not well-prepared. You want to make sure you have everything you need so you're not running out at the last minute to pick up "one more thing" from the store. AND a well-planned party will make you the hostess with the mostess (or the Host with the Most)!

Here's what you'll need to plan the perfect party:

Guests – Give your guests at least a few weeks' notice. Get the word out by phone, social media, email, or even old-fashioned paper invitations. Informal last-minute parties also work great, but if you're planning big, give your guests enough notice in advance to clear their calendars. Ask for an RSVP so you'll know how many guests to expect, but know that people are not always so great at responding. If it's a party that needs a specific count, such as a sit-down dinner, you may need to personally contact each guest who hasn't replied.

Food – Things don't have to be fancy or expensive to make a party a success. But whether it's elaborate or simplistic, nobody likes a party where there's not enough food!

You can (1) buy or prepare all of the food yourself, (2) ask guests to pitch in, or (3) have it catered. Whatever you decide, here are a few tips and guidelines:

* Offer a variety (sweet, salty, hot, cold, heavy, light) and consider guests' dietary restrictions.

* If you're doing it yourself, write out a backwards timeline for food preparation and do as much as you can ahead of time.

* If the party is at a traditional meal time, guests will likely expect heavier food. If the meal is not immediately served when guests arrive, plan to have snacks or hors d'oeuvres available.

* As you think through your menu, plan how you will serve the food. You'll need a serving dish and specific utensil for each item.

Drinks — Consider coffee, tea, soft drinks, beer or wine, juice or punch, etc.

Ice — Even if drinks are already chilled, many people like to have ice. Also, consider how you will serve the ice.

Serving ware (plates, cups, napkins, forks, spoons, knives, etc.) — Serving a meal? You'll need big plates. Dessert? Small plates. Meat? You'll need knives. Cups or glasses for each type of beverage offered — for example, if you offer coffee, you'll need a cup that can hold a hot beverage. For snack or dessert plates, plan that each guest may use more than one.

Seating — If it's not a seated event, you don't have to have one chair per person, as some people will mingle and be up and down. If you're planning a traditional meal, though, you'll need enough tables and chairs for every guest to be seated. There are businesses that rent out tables and chairs if you don't have enough.

Decorations — Decorations are optional, but you'll want to think this through ahead of time. Is there a theme? Do you need flowers? Balloons? Centerpieces? Tablecloths? Streamers? Banners? If you're having a formal party, you may want to rent or buy tablecloths and cloth napkins.

Activity — Are you going to have music? Games? Swimming? A fire pit? Movie night? A band and dancing? If your plan is to simply hang out, it's still good to have something planned in case there's a lull in the conversation.

Do the thing today that you wish you would have already done. This time next week, you will have done it!

— Laura Thomae Young

– 10 –

ADULTING WITH YOUR MONEY

"Most money problems are a result of inattention."

"Is there anything you feel you should have learned in school that you don't know?"

I have interviewed dozens of young women and asked them this question. Almost everyone answered, "Finances."

Staying on top of your finances and taking care of your money is one of the Hard Things, but it's a skill that can be learned and a discipline that pays off from the very first day you begin working at it.

Most money problems are a result of *inattention*. Making a budget and sticking to it sounds too hard and complicated, so it's tempting to just pay the bills and hope there's some left over. Debt creeps up and up and up as we satisfy the craving to have more and have more now.

In this chapter, let's unravel some of the mystery of taking care of your money and work toward building a simple budget.

You may choose to go all in and get software and figure out your interest rates and learn investing and delve deep into the financial world, but that's certainly not what we're going to do here. My goal is to make it simple to understand and even simpler to do.

If you're starting anything new, know that the more complicated you make it, the less likely you are to follow through. A plain and simple budget that you'll actually stick to is one thousand times better than a complicated one that never sees the light of day.

I want to make a HUGE disclaimer that I'm not an expert in finances or money. Raising four children on a single-income minister's budget for more than twenty years (I was a stay-at-home mom when my kids were small), we always struggled with money. Usually the problem was "not enough," but we also racked up some debt and made some financial mistakes that plague us still today. So, I come to this with a bit of experience from both the positive and the negative side.

I have five steps for you to work through that will change your financial life. The steps are simple, but not easy. What I mean by that is that it's not a *complicated* process, and anyone can do it, but it's sticking to it that can make it hard.

The process is going to be work, but it will be worth it

This is definitely in the category of doing Hard Things now that make life easier later – and taking the easy way out is really going to make life hard hard hard later.

If you're like me, you might be a little afraid of what you'll find if you go through these steps, but trust me that it's much better to be bummed out and informed than to be blissfully ignorant.

You can use old-fashioned paper to write out your budget, or you can do this on an electronic worksheet. Either way, the steps are going to be the same and you're going to see where you are.

Okay, ready to buckle down and get started?

- Figure out what your income is.
- Figure out what your out-go is.
- Set aside some money for emergencies.
- Make a plan for getting out of debt, (if you have debt).
- Save up for a Rainy Day, your Retirement, and Big Future Purchases.

Step One – Figure out what your income is

If you have one job and get paid a fixed amount either weekly, every two weeks, or monthly, then this step may be an easy exercise. If you work on commission, are an entrepreneur, work for tips, or have any other irregular income, use your average monthly income. If your income is seasonal, unless you're already in the habit of saving up during the

Adulting Like a Boss

"high" season for the lean times, I suggest using the average income you receive during the low season for this exercise.

> **A plain and simple budget that you'll actually stick to is one thousand times better than a complicated one that never sees the light of day.**

Think through any other income you get regularly – any side biz, weekend jobs, alimony, child support, trust fund, monthly check from Great Aunt Louise, or investment dividends. If you have income that comes in sporadically but not regularly, let's put a pin in that for now. For this exercise, just figure out what you can always count on, month over month.

If you get paid twice a month, you probably get a regular check on a certain day of the month, such as the first and the fifteenth. Most companies will pay the Friday before, if payday occurs on a weekend. Getting paid twice a month will mean getting 24 paychecks per year.

12 months x 2 paychecks = 24 paychecks

If you get paid every other week, you'll be getting 26 paychecks per year.

52 divided by 2 = 26 paychecks

We are going to base this exercise on a monthly budget, so if you're getting paid every other week, there will be two months during the year that you'll actually be receiving *three* checks. We're not going to count the third odd paycheck that comes twice per year. You can use it for saving up for something or paying down a debt and just think of it as "gravy."

Whether your annual pay is divided into 24 payments or 26 payments won't change the amount, just how it is divided out.

You'll be subtracting everything that comes *out* of your paycheck, so make sure the number reflects the gross income. (Gross income is the amount before anything is subtracted.)

Check out the *Adulting Like a Boss* website for your own free budget worksheet! http://www.Adultinglikeaboss.net/freebies

Now that you have a number in front of you, let's figure out where that money goes.

Step Two — Figure out what your out-go is

If you are a full-time employee, your taxes should be taken out before you receive your check. Most corporate jobs have automatic deductions (subtractions) for federal and state taxes and other things like insurance.

Assuming you have direct deposit, as most people do, your company should have a website where you can see your pay. The pay stub (still called the pay stub because it used to be part of a paper check) is where it shows what you make, what has been taken out, and the remainder being deposited into your account.

It's good for you to write out what you're paying in taxes, because you need to know. Everyone should be aware of how much and what kind of taxes they are paying.

Insurance is another expense you likely have if you are working for a company of any significant size. Look at your pay stub and see what kinds of insurance are being taken out. Usually there is some choice about what insurance you get, and you should be aware of your options.

Now once you've figured out what comes regularly out of your paycheck, you should see on your paystub what your bring-home-pay is. This is the number we'll be working with through the rest of the exercise.

Using the worksheet, write down every single expense you have, putting each item under the appropriate category.

Some expenses will be regular – car payments, student loans, some utilities, phone, cable. There are others that vary.

> **The emergency fund has eased my mind more than anything else I've done with my money.**

Use the average monthly expense for the expenses that vary. Some expenses, like car maintenance, you may only have occasionally. You'll want to have a category for things like that so you're saving up for when those expenses come.

For the expenses that vary from week to week and month to month, you may have to work to figure this out.

There are four suggested methods for finding out what you normally spend on things that vary – groceries and eating out are good examples. You may not be able to do this without some serious digging through your finances, and this step could take a week or even a month, but stick with it! It's worth the trouble!

App method – Several budget apps that link your spending with categories are available to access on your phone. Many banks have an app that will link to your card, or there are separate apps that you can download and link to your spending. The way one of these apps works is that every time you go to the grocery store, for example, once you've put that particular store into the "grocery" category, the app will track it. If you use a bank card rather than cash, (like most people,) this is the easiest way to track your spending.

Receipt method – For everything you buy, either keep the receipt or write it down. Keep a small notebook and write down every single purchase – from the cup of coffee at Starbucks to the weekly grocery bill.

Cash method – Put some cash in an envelope and mark on the outside of the envelope the category and the amount you put in. For example, put $50 into an envelope and write "Eat Out - $50" on the outside. If you need to replenish the envelope, write the additional amount on the outside of the envelope as you replenish. (You may want to do this to keep from carrying around too much cash, also). Don't spend any money that isn't in the envelope. At the end of the month, you'll know how much you spent on eating out by how much cash you've gone through.

Bank statement method – Go to your online banking site and look through your records. Every transaction should be listed for the month, and you can figure out what you've spent in each category by the name of the establishment.

In this exercise, you aren't yet figuring out what your out-go *should* be, but what it actually is. Be honest with yourself and write down everything you are spending. Don't forget to enter the little things – a quick lunch, coffee, movies. This exercise is meant to help you see where your money goes.

Also, don't judge yourself! This exercise is like taking your temperature. The medicine will come later!

Step Three — Set some money aside for emergencies

Despite any debt, negative bank balance, beautiful somethings that you've just GOT to have, save up $1,000 and put it somewhere you can get to easily if there's an emergency. A TRUE emergency.

What constitutes as an emergency? A car that has to be fixed so you can get to work that exceeds your planned budget. A broken refrigerator. A burst hot water heater (if you own and don't rent). A sick loved one who lives far away. It's something that you don't have the funds saved up for – that you didn't or couldn't possibly have planned for.

> **One of the first rules of trying to get out of debt is this: Stop accumulating more debt. If you are a credit card junkie, STOP!**

This is *not* a savings account for purchases (unless your purchase is an emergency). It's not to pull out for a last-minute invitation for a fun trip. It's only to be used for a true emergency.

A few ideas for squirreling this money away:

- **Freeze it** – Put the cash into a plastic bag and freeze it into a block of ice.
- **Frame it** – Put it into a picture frame that's hard to open, (with a picture on top) and hang it up.
- **Hide it** – Put it at a family member's house (with permission) in a safe location.
- **Bank it** – Put it into a savings account that is separate from any other accounts and don't get a bank card – or you can put the

bank card, rather than the cash, into one of the places mentioned above.

Whatever you do, don't give yourself easy access. This money is to give you peace of mind if anything unexpected happens. If you end up needing it, replace it as quickly as possible.

It may take you some time to save up $1,000 to put away, but make it a priority. This will help you budget the rest of your money with a different attitude. You don't have to wait until you have the full $1,000 to put an emergency fund aside. You may want to start with $100 and add to it as you can.

The emergency fund has eased my mind more than anything else I've done with my money.

Step Four – Make a plan for getting out of debt, if you have debt

One of the first rules of trying to get out of debt is this: Stop accumulating more debt. If you are a credit card junkie, *stop*.

Some financial gurus will tell you to only get loans for the purchase of a house, and everything else will be cash only. I think it's realistic to also plan that you'll have student loans, since many people do, as well as (possibly) car payments. Any other debts should be on your list to pay off and not borrow anymore for.

Medical or dental bills are also something you may have to pay over time, since they typically come unexpectedly and can quickly exceed your budgeted plan.

Vacations, clothing, eating out, and your basic household bills should be paid with money you have in your bank account.

If you find you are not able to meet your bills each month, you have two choices: Either you have to lower your bills or raise your income.

- **Lowering your bills** can mean moving to a place that's less expensive to live, getting a roommate, changing your lifestyle and living more simply and frugally.
- **Raising your income** can mean finding a better paying job, getting a second job, having a side hustle that brings in money, or selling things of your own to bring in money.

I hope it goes without saying that more loans are not what fixes financial problems. Quick loans, payday loans, and any other kind of "Get Cash Quick" loans are a terrible idea. The interest rate is astronomical and they get you into a perpetual cycle of debt that is very difficult to overcome.

Your car: Some financial gurus will tell you to only pay cash for a car. The idea is to drive a "junker" until you can pay cash for a better car. Then drive that better car, making car payments to yourself, and sell the second car, using the savings to buy an even better car for cash, and so forth, until you get a car you really want and have paid for it in cash. That's a great way to pay cash for a car, and keep "trading up" until you get the car you really want.

> Quick loans, payday loans, and any other kind of "Get Cash Quick" loans are a terrible idea.

When I tried this method a few years back, though, I made the mistake of going too low in quality, and my "junker" constantly had mechanical problems. The repair bills ended up being more than what the car was worth. If the junker isn't dependable or is having constant problems, it's not realistic. The car payments I was supposed to be making to myself went instead to the mechanic.

Nobody wants a car loan, but for me, it was a better choice to buy a nicer, but slightly used car with a repair warranty, and have a predictable car note, that I was counting on each month. Driving my low-quality junker, I would cringe each time the car wouldn't start or made a funny noise, knowing I was sinking more money into repairs for a car that probably wasn't even worth the cost of the repair.

If you are fortunate enough to have the financial means to pay cash for a car without a loan, that is definitely the right thing to do. Having a big car debt will weigh you down. If you do need to borrow for a car, however, buy a dependable car that is within your budget, with payments you can easily afford each month, and pay it off as quickly as possible.

Step Five — Save up for a Rainy Day, your Retirement, and Big Future Purchases

After you've gotten yourself on a budget, have saved up a little emergency money, and are Adulting Like a Boss with your day-to-day decisions about your money, it's time to start thinking about the big things.

If your employer has a 401K, you should definitely participate, especially if it's a matching 401K. A 401K is a savings plan that employers offer. It pulls money out of your pay and puts it into a savings

Adulting Like a Boss

account, and you are not taxed on that money unless you pull it out of the 401K. A matching 401K means that whatever you pledge to put into the savings account, your employer will match all or part of it. Most people put 3-6% of their gross pay into their 401K, and some companies will match the entire amount.

Retirement may seem light years away, but when you're in your twenties, that works in your favor. Saving just a little each month will pile up a nice chunk of change down the road.

You also might want to begin saving several months' worth of your salary and putting it aside as a just-in-case fund. That may take some time, but it will give you great peace of mind. In that case, if anything happens to your job, you don't have to freak out – at least not immediately.

> **Retirement may seem light years away, but when you're in your twenties, that works in your favor. Saving just a little each month will pile up a nice chunk of change down the road.**

Money money money – it's something we all have to deal with. It doesn't have to be unpleasant or overwhelming, and it certainly doesn't have to be complicated. Following through with your commitments will be the hardest part, but remember, it's the hard stuff that makes life easier in the long run.

Next Steps

After you've gotten yourself on a budget, you may want to talk to a financial counselor about investments – how to best save and guard your money to get the most out of it. This simple plan I've presented is just the basics of getting yourself out of debt and on a budget so you know where you are financially and you are making wise use of your money.

HOW TO...

Find a Bargain and Save Money on Everyday Purchases

If you're on a tight budget or even if you have some money to burn, you want to spend the minimum on products you buy repeatedly. It's a good idea to find out where you can buy those items for the best bargain. Here's a quick process to help you save money on everyday items:

1. Make a tracker list of items you purchase consistently, such as paper products, cleaning products, food staples like bread, milk, cheese, etc.. Get your free worksheet at:

    www.Adultinglikeaboss.net/freebies

2. Print out the list, or save it on your phone, and have it in hand for the next few weeks. Each time you shop, try a different store. Keep track of how much each of these items cost. Make notes if this is an item that is regularly marked down. Try stores you don't normally frequent, as well as dollar stores, big box stores, and pharmacies.

3. Try out the store's brand for some of these items. Sometimes they are just as good as the more expensive name brands – but sometimes not. You just need to try it to see. Read online reviews of products and brands before buying, so you don't waste money on a product that may not serve you well.

4. Check weekly ads for coupons. Coupon-clipping can be helpful, especially if a store doubles them. But don't get carried away – you need to figure out if it's worth the time it takes to save a dollar or two.

5. Check online prices. You may be able to find equal prices by ordering your items online and having them delivered. This potentially saves you time and money from going into a store and possibly coming home with more items that were not on your list to begin with.

You probably don't have the time or the desire to run all over town hunting for bargains. After the exercise of shopping at several stores, note which one has the overall best savings and shop there regularly.

Sooner rather than later!

— Laura Thomae Young

– 11 –

ADULTING WITH YOUR TAXES

"When payday finally came, I took one look at my check and boy was I disappointed! Where in the heck was all my money?"

In the tenth grade, I got my first real job – wrapping Christmas presents at a sporting goods store. I wasn't getting paid much more than minimum wage, but I was excited about the money I'd be receiving in my first paycheck to buy Christmas gifts for my family with my very own money.

I carefully figured out exactly how much I was earning, multiplied it by the hours I was working, and knew exactly how much I would have on my check.

Of course, when payday finally came, I took one look at my check (a paper check in those days) and boy was I disappointed! Where in the heck was all my money? Had I misunderstood how much I was earning? Had I multiplied wrong? Had my employer cheated me?

> **Taxes don't really have to be all that complicated.**

Nope, none of the above. It was the first time I heard those dirty little words – *payroll taxes*! I hadn't known to take into account that each time I earned a dollar, my employer would take a piece of that dollar and send it to the government on my behalf.

I've interviewed dozens of young men and women over the last year, asking what gaps they have in "Adulting." Many have expressed the same things: They don't understand how taxes and withholdings work, they don't feel confident filling out tax forms, and they aren't sure what to do when it comes time to file taxes.

Taxes can seem confusing, but if you are a single person who is only financially responsible for yourself, and you're earning a paycheck from a company, taxes don't really have to be all that complicated.

Disclaimer: I am not an expert in finance nor is this by any means an exhaustive look at taxes. I want to give only a basic overview and equip you with a working knowledge of how the system works.

It's true that taxes take a chunk of money from your paycheck, but for good reason. Your taxes pay for things like public schools, roads and bridges, police and fire departments, military, government salaries, libraries and museums, and funding for public services. Although it is the government who takes these taxes from your paycheck, all taxes are either voted upon directly by registered voters or the elected officials who represent them. For those of us living in the United States of America, "the government" is you.

Some of this information may not apply if you are an independent contractor or self-employed, because the paperwork is a little bit different. For the sake of this chapter, however, I am addressing those who work for a company and get paid as employees.

The most confusing part is the terminology

Once you understand the vocabulary, much of the muddle fades away.

The ***Internal Revenue Service (IRS)*** is the government entity that handles federal taxes. To report your income and pay your taxes, you are required to fill out a few forms (more about those later) and turn them in. April 15th is the date set to submit your information, or *file your tax return*, for the previous year's income.

A little terminology about your pay.

- **Gross pay** – Your entire pay before anything is taken out.
- **Net pay** – The pay you actually bring home.
- **Taxable income** – The part of your pay that is taxed by the state and federal government. (There are some things that may make part of your pay non-taxable.)

As with any government or legal transaction, there are papers you are responsible to fill out with words you may not use in any other walk of life. Below are the basic forms you'll see, and I've highlighted some of the terms that can cause confusion.

Starting with the basics - the forms

There are many many forms that the IRS has for every conceivable situation. For the purpose of this exercise, we are going to look at three forms that are pertinent for you to understand your income tax: The W-4, the W-2, and the 1040.

W-4 – You fill it out at your new job

The W-4 is the form you fill out for your employer when you first get a job. You have to fill this out within the first couple of days of working, because it lets your employer know how much tax to take out of your paycheck. This form does not get turned in to the government, only to your employer.

Your employer has a table that shows them exactly how much tax to take from your paycheck, according to how you filled out the W-4. Then the employer pays your taxes on your behalf. That way,

> Your taxes pay for things like public schools, roads and bridges, police and fire departments, military, government salaries, libraries and museums, and funding for public services.

you are not responsible for a big tax bill when you file your yearly taxes.

It is important to fill the W-4 out accurately. If you pay too little tax throughout the year, you'll owe the IRS money, and possibly even have to pay a penalty for not having paid enough. If you pay too much, you'll get a tax refund.

I had a sudden flash of adultness when I realized I was running my business as an artist full time and actually paying all my bills.
--Betsy M – 24

A lot of people like getting a tax refund and view it as a big yearly bonus. However, getting a refund means that you basically loaned the government your hard-earned money for twelve months with no interest. Think about this - wouldn't you rather have had that money throughout the year and brought home a bigger paycheck?

The W-4 is a two-page document, but the part you fill out for your employer is about half a page long. The rest of it is a worksheet to help you figure out what to put on the half page. The worksheet asks questions about your life situation - if you're single, married, filing your taxes individually, or as a couple, along with questions about any *dependents* (people for whom you are financially responsible, for example, if you have children).

The worksheet translates the answers to those questions into *claimed allowances*. The number of *allowances* determines how much federal tax is taken out of your paycheck each pay period. The more allowances you end up with, the less money is taken out.

Adulting Like a Boss

If you're single with no dependents, the worksheet will prompt you with only a couple of allowances. If you have dependents or are planning to file your taxes jointly with your spouse, the worksheet will prompt you accordingly. You can see the worksheet on the IRS site: https://www.irs.gov/pub/irs-pdf/fw4.pdf.

You can change the allowances at any time by filling out a new W-4 and turning it in to your employer. If you got a big refund last year and not much has changed since that time, you may want to change your allowances. Talk to your employer about refiguring your allowances so you'll come out about even next year.

Any time you have a life event, such as marriage or the birth of a child, you should re-do the worksheet and make changes to your W-4. The more people you have who are dependent on you, the more allowances you can take.

If you have state income taxes, you'll fill out a similar, but separate form for the state. However, we are going to stick to talking about federal taxes in this chapter.

W-2 – Your employer gives it to you at the end of the year

The W-2 is a form your employer provides you, indicating what you made the previous year and what federal income tax was withheld. You have the option of getting it electronically only or a having a physical copy sent to your home address.

You'll need the W-2 when you file your income tax and a copy will be attached to your tax return. Your employer is required to send this to you by a date set by the IRS, usually by the end of January or first of February.

The W-2 also reports what amount of your income was subject to *Social Security tax* and *Medicare tax* and how much was paid. These two taxes are fixed percentage rates of your income and are split down the middle between you and your employer. At the time of this writing, the Social Security tax is 12.4% (so your part is 6.2%) and Medicare tax is 2.9% (so your part is 1.45%).

If you have a state or local income tax, the W-2 will also list how much was withheld for each of those.

1040 – You fill it out and submit it to the IRS every year

This is the form you fill out and turn in to the IRS by April 15th each year, reporting your previous year's income, any taxes still owed, overpayment of taxes (and a refund due to you), or if you broke even. There are a few versions of the 1040 for individuals, and according to what your situation is, you will need to use the one that is right for you. You can go to the IRS website and see the criteria for which form to use. https://www.irs.gov/taxtopics/tc352

You'll most likely file the 1040EZ form if:
- You are single
- You have an income of under $100,000
- You don't have other money to report
- You have no one else you are financially responsible for
- You are not going to itemize your deductions
- You haven't recently made any changes (buying a house, etc.)

But again, if you have any doubt, are filing for the first or second time, have had any changes or complexities with your financial situation, get a professional or at least an experienced family member or friend to help you.

Deductions

Although it is necessary for people to pay taxes to support and sustain a society, most people want to pay only what is required. Some of your income will be non-taxable through something called *tax deductions*. A *tax deduction* reduces your overall *taxable income*.

The IRS gives you a choice of either *itemizing* (listing them all out) any *deductions* that you are eligible for or taking one *standard deduction*.

The *standard deduction* is a set amount that you can subtract from your taxable income. If you don't itemize your deductions, you are eligible to take the standard deduction. The standard deduction is just good ol' Uncle Sam giving you a break on some of your money. In 2016, the standard deduction for a single person was $6,300.

> A tax deduction reduces your overall taxable income.

You should itemize deductions if they add up to be more than your standard deduction or if you don't qualify to use the standard deduction. Examples of *itemized deductions* are charitable donations, home mortgage interest, some medical expenses, or property taxes.

Adulting with Your Taxes

> For those of us living in the United States of America, "the government" is you.

Remember that a deduction is subtracted from your taxable income. For example, if you made $50,000 and took the standard deduction, it would reduce the amount of taxable income by $6,300. Then you would only pay taxes on $43,700.

Besides the standard deduction, you are also able to take (or *claim*) a *personal exemption*, another subtraction from the amount of your taxable income. If you have *dependents* (people for whom you are financially responsible) you claim an exemption for each of them too. For 2016, the personal exemption was $4,050. Again, it's Uncle Sam giving you a break from paying taxes on every single dollar you earn.

Using the same example of an income of $50,000, with both the standard deduction of $6,300 plus the additional personal exemption of $4,050, the taxable income would now be reduced to $39,650.

An added note: If someone else is claiming an exemption for you on their tax return, such as your spouse or your parents, you can't also claim yourself.

Tax Bracket

Once you have taken the exemptions and deductions, you are left with your *taxable income*. You only pay taxes on that amount. The amount you pay is then determined by *tax brackets*.

There are tax brackets for singles, couples filing jointly, couples filing separately, and heads of household. Below is the 2016 chart showing tax brackets for a single person. Each tax bracket includes two amounts: the base amount and the ceiling amount. Any of your taxable income that falls in between those two numbers is taxed at that bracket's rate. You are not taxed solely in *one* tax bracket (unless you make $9,275 or less annually), but multiple brackets.

According to the chart below, if you have $50,000 in taxable income, you would be taxed in *three* brackets. The first $9,275 would be taxed at 10%, then from $9,276 - $37,650 would be taxed at 15%, and the remainder of the $50,000 would be taxed at 25%.

Rate	Single
10%	Up to $9,275
15%	$9,276 – $37,650
25%	$37,651 – $91,150
28%	$91,151 – $190,150
33%	$190,151 – $413,350
35%	$413,351 – $415,050

When someone says they are "in the 25% tax bracket," it means their top taxable income falls into that bracket.

There's a myth that if you get a raise and make more money, you'll get put into a higher tax bracket and once you pay taxes on the higher salary, you could actually bring home less. You can see from the tax bracket chart above that the myth is not true. If you got a raise and your taxable income bumped into the next tax bracket, you would only pay a higher tax rate on the salary amount in that new bracket.

Final thoughts

Hopefully this clarifies some of the mystery around income taxes. When you get ready to file your tax return, I recommend you get a professional or a family member or friend with experience to help you through the first time or two. You can always try it on your own and get someone with experience to double-check your work.

> **If someone else is claiming an exemption for you on their tax return, such as your spouse or your parents, you can't also claim yourself.**

Paying a professional can be worth the trouble and cost, and around tax time, you'll find many pop-up companies who can help you if your finances are simple – like if you're single with one job and no dependents. If you have multiple jobs, have changed jobs a few times, have other income besides your paycheck from your job, want to itemize your deductions, have recently purchased a house, or other factors that may make it more complex, I encourage you to consult a tax accountant.

Sometimes the hard thing might only take five minutes.

— Laura Thomae Young

– 12 –

ADULTING LIKE A HOMEOWNER – THE MONEY PART

*"A good realtor is working to help you.
Find one you can trust and then... trust them!"*

You have to live somewhere and, unless you're living rent free with mom and dad, you'll have to pay for where you live. Buying a house is a big decision and might be right for you. First, let me tell you that I'm not an expert on real estate or mortgages, and this is not an exhaustive dissertation on buying a house. I definitely recommend that you talk to family and friends who are homeowners and to professionals, like realtors and mortgage lenders.

This is a good overview, however, if you're a complete newbie. Be warned: There's a whole new vocabulary with words you may never use again after the house-buying phase(s) of your life.

Two important people in the process

If you're buying your first home, you'll need a team of experienced professionals who can walk you through the process.

> You need someone with experience to walk you through one of the biggest life decisions you'll make.

The lender.

A mortgage lender will be the person who helps you get a loan for the purchase of the home you want to buy. Ask family, friends, or co-workers who have purchased a home whom they would recommend. Your bank is also a good place to obtain your loan, if you've been pleased with your banking business. If you've already contacted a realtor, he or she will be able to recommend reputable lenders.

Since you're a newbie at this, make sure you find someone with experience and a good reputation. A lender should not ask for any money up front. Lenders get paid by commission on deals they close, so they are highly motivated to work with you and make the purchase happen. Only after you have found a house you are serious about buying will there be any fees to pay, and those fees will be clearly outlined.

A word of caution about finding a lender - choose someone local you can meet with face to face. Internet lenders, who get paid by the hour, aren't going to care as much about your best interest.

The real estate agent, your new best friend.

A realtor (also known as a real estate agent) is the person who will show you properties, write your offer on a house, and get you to the closing table. If you are a first time home buyer, you don't have experience. You shouldn't get a realtor who also doesn't have experience. If your best friend has just gotten her real estate license and wants you to help her get started, don't. Take her out to dinner and give her a thumbs up and an "Atta' girl!"...but you need someone with experience to walk you through one of the biggest life decisions you'll make.

Ask family, friends, and coworkers who have recently bought a house if they recommend you use their realtor. If you've already found a lender, they will also be able to recommend a few realtors. Meet with several and choose someone you like and trust. Realtors, like lenders, only get paid on commission when they help someone buy or sell a property, so there's no cost to you to engage a realtor.

Even though you may balk at the idea of paying someone to help you buy something, buying a house is a complex process, and if you're inexperienced, you don't want to try to do it yourself. Even if you are buying a home that is "For Sale By Owner," a realtor can help you avoid pitfalls. A good realtor is working to help you. Find one you can trust and then… trust them!

Don't be surprised if older, more experienced realtors don't have a strong online presence. Good realtors who have worked in the area and have a strong reputation will count on word-of-mouth and personal referrals for most of their business.

> "Either you're paying your own mortgage, or you're paying someone else's."

Once you've decided on a realtor, you may be asked to sign an agreement with them. It's a commitment to work exclusively with that one person. Even if there isn't a signed agreement, it's an unspoken rule that you only work with one. If you become unhappy with a realtor for any reason, you can ask to get out of the agreement. For realtors, it's unethical for them to work with a client who already has a commitment to another realtor (stealing clients).

Buying vs. Renting

Like most things in life that push you toward a decision, there are pros and cons to buying a house. Several realtors I interviewed while researching this chapter shared with me the same quote: "Either you're paying your own mortgage, or you're paying someone else's." In other words, if you're renting, you're helping your landlord pay the mortgage of the rental property you are occupying.

It's not unusual to be paying about the same amount monthly in rent that you would be paying on a mortgage for your own house. When paying rent, though, you don't have anything to show for it at the end of your time in the home. If you're paying a mortgage, you are building **equity**.

A home is a financial investment, and a rent payment is money that's paid and gone forever.

On the other hand, if the water heater bursts and your basement is flooded, if a tree falls on the house, or the AC breaks, as a homeowner you are responsible to get it fixed. There's no landlord you can call. It's up to you to take the responsibility of time, trouble, and expense for repairs and maintenance.

If you're new to an area, it's a good idea to rent for a while – about six to twelve months – to really know the area before you decide to buy. What initially may look like a part of town you want to live in may end up being undesirable once you're settled in and know the city.

> A home is a financial investment, and a rent payment is money that's paid and gone forever.

Tax advantage.

A financial advantage of buying a home is the tax break. You can deduct (subtract) mortgage interest (explained below), property taxes, and some of the expenses of the purchase from your total taxable income. What this means is that it will lower the amount of your income that you are taxed on, and can result in lowering your tax bracket. (Remember, we went over this in the last chapter? See p. 125.)

In that sense, it's almost like Uncle Sam is paying part of your mortgage payment. When you buy a home, you'll need to talk to an accountant to see how much tax write-off you'll have. Unless you're a tax whiz, you need to get an accountant to do your taxes – at least for the year that you purchase your new home, as the taxes will be a little more complicated.

When to buy

You shouldn't buy a house until you are financially stable with regular income. Getting on a budget and sticking with it is an important step in that direction (see chapter 10). You'll need money for a down payment and closing costs, (more about that later). Even if you're not planning on buying a house right away, start saving up for those things. The cost of the purchase transaction is a big expense, (in other words, you have to pay a bunch of stuff when you first buy the house) but after that, it's not unusual for your monthly mortgage payment to be about equal to what you'd pay in rent.

Step 1 — Understand the financial aspect

The first thing to do before looking at houses is to find out how much house you can afford. You don't want to find your dream home and then discover it is out of your price range. It doesn't cost anything to meet with a mortgage lender and get pre-approved for a loan. (If you're one of the lucky few who have the means to pay cash for a house, you can skip this step!)

There are all types of loans, and a lender can explain the advantages and disadvantages of each. They'll look at your income, your credit score, and your debt. Even if you're not in a great place financially, most reputable lenders will give you all kinds of ideas on reducing your overall debt and raising your credit score to qualify for a better loan. The better financial shape you're in, the lower interest rates you'll be able to qualify for.

Credit score.

Your credit score will come into play at this point, so know what it is, and work toward improving it by paying off or paying down debts. You don't have to be completely out of debt, but your debt will count against you when you try to borrow for a house.

If you don't have any debts and haven't ever borrowed, talk to your banker about ways you can build your credit score. Usually a credit card that you make a few purchases on and pay off each month will help build your score, but again, talk with your banker, an accountant, or the mortgage lender.

> What initially may look like a part of town you want to live in may end up being undesirable once you're settled in and know the city.

Besides your credit score, your lender will also look at your credit history. You may have a great (or terrible) score because you haven't had but a handful of loans.

Personal finances.

After you've put yourself on a budget and stuck with it for several months, you may be ready to start house hunting. You'll have a better idea of what you'll really be able to afford, and you'll have the amount you've been approved for.

There's more to a mortgage than just the cost of the house, so talk with a lender to make sure you understand what your house payment would be. Unless you have a good grasp of mortgages and all they entail, don't try to figure it out yourself.

You'll need to have money for a down payment, money to pay closing costs (usually but not always), and it's a good idea to have about three months of personal expenses saved up, just in case something happens with your job – you don't want to lose your house. That would give you enough cushion to get by until you figure out your life situation.

Understanding the mortgage payment.

There are four items built into your monthly payment: principal, interest, taxes and insurance (PITI). The **principal**, as in any loan, is the actual money you're borrowing. The **interest** is the price you pay for borrowing that money. The first few years of a loan, your monthly payment is more interest than principal. The **taxes** are property taxes. The **insurance** is homeowner's insurance (in case your house burns down), and for certain kinds of loans there will also be mortgage insurance (for the lender's protection in case you can't pay your loan).

You can ask your lender for an **Amortization Schedule**, which is a detailed look at what portion of each mortgage payment goes toward each component of PITI.

Within the loan there is normally an **escrow account**, which is an account the lender keeps to pay your insurance and taxes on the home. Each month, your payment includes all four items listed above, and the insurance and taxes are put into the escrow account. When insurance and taxes come due each year, the money has been set aside and the lender pays them from that account. There may be slight changes to insurance and taxes from time to time that will slightly affect your monthly payment.

Down payments and loans.

A mortgage lender will determine what kind of loan you qualify for, how much money you can borrow, and about how much you'd need for a down payment, (the cash you pay up front).

One kind of loan, called a conventional loan, requires a down payment of about 20% of the purchase price. If that's discouraging to you, because you think you'll never be able to save

> **There are four items built into your monthly payment:**
> 1. principal
> 2. interest
> 3. taxes
> 4. insurance

up that much, don't despair. Other types of loans require even as little as 3.5% down. Your lender will help find a loan that's right for you. Most home loans are 30-year loans, but if you have a big down payment and can afford a heftier monthly payment, you'll pay much less interest with a 15-year loan.

Ideally, you want a conventional loan in order to get the lowest interest rate. For that type of loan, your credit score should be 700 or above. Because you are paying 20% down, you don't have to have mortgage insurance. That's a good thing because mortgage insurance is one of the things that's rolled into your mortgage payment.

A common type of loan for first-time home buyers is an FHA loan, and the minimum credit score to qualify is 580 at the time of this writing. It's a loan backed by the government that was first introduced to stimulate the economy because it gives people with less means an opportunity to buy houses. An FHA loan usually only requires about 3.5% down.

If you're a veteran, you likely qualify for a VA loan, which is a great option. Be sure and let your lender know if you're a veteran and they can see if you qualify.

Closing costs.

Besides your down payment, be ready to pay an additional chunk of money for closing costs. Closing costs vary greatly and depend on the property you are buying, the type of loan you are getting, and other factors.

Closing costs cover fees for processing papers involved with the loan, credit reports, and a few other things that all add up. They will also include a title search, making sure the property is properly owned by the person selling it, that there are no heirs of previous owners laying claim to it, or that there are no liens against the property. A lien is legal action to collect owed money from the owner, and a property can't be sold until that debt is settled.

It's important to have a realtor and lender you trust, because there will be fees you've never heard of and you'll need to pay them to finish the deal. Do your research and see what fees you'll be required to pay at closing, because they depend on several factors.

In some cases, a seller who is eager to unload their property will be willing to pay part or all of the closing costs, but most often this is the responsibility of the buyer.

Before the day of the closing you'll receive an estimate of the cost, but you likely won't know the exact amount until it's all figured out that day.

Be prepared for closing costs to be between 2% and 5% of the cost of the house. It's not a set percentage, but it's all those fees added up. In some cases, the closing costs are rolled into the loan, but that means more money you're borrowing and a higher monthly payment.

> **In some cases, a seller who is eager to unload their property will be willing to pay part or all of the closing costs, but most often this is the responsibility of the buyer.**

Step 2 — Understand the market

One thing to keep in mind is that every market is different. Here in Nashville, at the time of this writing, it's a "seller's market," which means that homes are selling like hotcakes and a seller has multiple offers to choose from. Houses don't stay on the market for long and if you find a house you like, you have to act fast and understand that you're competing with other people who also want to buy it.

In the town my mom lives in, however, there are more homes for sale than there are people looking to buy. Because of that, a seller may be willing to do whatever they can to help close the deal. That's called a "buyer's market," because a buyer is in a good position to offer less money and ask for more from the seller in the negotiations, such as paying some of the closing costs.

If you're buying in a booming economy like Nashville, any house you purchase is likely to appreciate (or go up) in value over time. If you're in a depressed economy, the opposite is true. That's something to consider if you think you'll only be in an area for a limited number of years.

Although it may still be a good idea to buy versus rent, it may not be a financial growth investment.

The time of year you buy can also make a difference in negotiations. During the winter months, November, December, and January, not as many people are buying homes. Because of that, you may meet a desperate seller who is willing to come down on price or pay part of the closing costs.

Now that you know all about the money part, let's move on to the fun part – finding your perfect house!

HOW TO...

Boil a Perfect Egg That's Neither Gooey nor Green

Start by choosing eggs that have been in the fridge for a few days — they're easier to peel than fresh eggs!

1. Place a few eggs in a small boiler. Fill with water until the eggs are fully submerged. Turn on high heat and bring the water to a boil.
2. When the water comes to a rolling boil, cover with a lid and turn the heat off.
3. Let the eggs sit in the water for 15 minutes. Then, drain the hot water from the eggs and run cold water over them. Cooking the eggs any longer or even letting them continue to sit in the hot water will cause the yolks to have a green halo around them.

If you're not going to eat the eggs right away, dry them, and use a pencil to write a big "B" on the shell, so you'll know it's a boiled egg. Store your boiled eggs in the fridge. They'll stay fresh and ready to eat for up to a week.

Take time to make your house a home. Decorate. Hang curtains. Plant flowers.

— Laura Thomae Young

– 13 –
ADULTING LIKE A HOMEOWNER – THE HOUSE PART

"Unless you are handy with tools and can do repairs yourself, stay away from the fixer-uppers."

When it comes to buying a house, there are three things that matter most: location, location, and location. It will matter much more about where the house is located than if it has a bay window or a fireplace. If you hate your commute, don't like the neighborhood, or wish you were rural when you are urban, you'll end up not liking even the most perfect house.

Adulting Like a Boss

From your meeting with the lender, you should be pre-approved for a loan, have an idea of down payments and closing costs, and know what monthly mortgage to expect for homes within a certain price range. Share all that information with your realtor so they will know what price range you can afford and keep you both from wasting time seeing houses that aren't going to work for your budget.

First — the neighborhood

You may want to go online on your own to find houses you'd like to see on websites like www.zillow.com or www.trulia.com (though they may not always be accurate), and your realtor should send you listings to preview before you go out to see them in person. I recommend driving by a house before you ask your realtor to show it to you. If you don't like the location, don't bother looking inside.

> **Drive through the neighborhood on a weekend and see your potential future neighbors.**

Drive through neighborhoods with houses in your price range. Do the drive to and from the area to your job at the same times you would be commuting each day to know what traffic would be like. Drive through the neighborhood on a weekend and see your potential future neighbors as they mow their lawn, rake their yards, or play with their kids outdoors. Stop and ask them how they like the neighborhood.

Look at crime statistics at www.Crimereports.com. Realtors are not allowed to "steer" people to or away from a neighborhood or tell you that a sex offender lives next door. They can only tell you to look at crime statistics.

Next — the house

Be as specific as you can to your realtor in describing what you have in mind. If you don't like a house that has been suggested, explain what you don't like. That way, your realtor can narrow down the search. A good realtor will ask you lots of questions or have you fill out a questionnaire to get a feel for what you're looking for. You may not realize what things you like or dislike until you've looked at a few houses.

> **Respect your realtor's time and limit the number of houses you go see to those you are truly interested in.**

Respect your realtor's time and limit the number of houses you go see to those you are truly interested in. If your realtor suggests a house you don't particularly want to see, let them know. They are not getting paid by the hour, but only receive the commission when you buy a house. Don't send them on a wild goose chase showing you house after house that isn't even within your consideration.

A lender may tell you how much you can afford, but you are the one who has to make that payment each month. You want to buy something you know you can afford month after month. With that in mind, consider buying a little more house than you need right now. If your life situation changes and you go from single to married, or from no kids to some kids, you'll be glad you have a house than can grow with you. Meanwhile, you can get a roommate and collect rent from them to help with the bigger mortgage or even use the extra bedroom for an Air B&B.

Speaking of kids, if you think you may be having kids in the future (or already have them), then the school district matters, so spend some time checking out the local schools your kids would be zoned for.

> *I knew I was really grown up when I finally learned the difference between subsidized and unsubsidized loans! You think you're grown and you have it all together, but then there are all those student loans. I wanted to defer the loans, but I finally realized, these were real loans that I really had to pay back!*
> *--Erica M – 31*

Unless you are handy with tools and can do repairs yourself, stay away from the fixer-uppers. My experience has been that every home repair or renovation turns into more time and money than originally estimated. A fresh coat of paint or new carpet is one thing (yes, yes, I know… technically those are two things), but ripping out and remodeling a bathroom is quite another.

When you're looking at houses that are occupied, you're free to open closets and cabinets and poke around a bit, but realize that you are walking through someone's private home. Even though they have the house on display, they still live there. Be respectful and don't touch their belongings. Plus sometimes owners have hidden cameras when their house is being shown. Most owners will leave the house for a showing, but occasionally they will be in the home. Don't show your enthusiasm if you love the house. If the owner knows you will buy the house no matter what, that gives you less negotiating power.

The offer and negotiations

Once you've found a house that will satisfy your needs and (hopefully) some of your wants, you and your realtor will present a written offer. The house will have a listed price, and how much you offer will depend on many factors, including how long the house has been for sale, what condition the house is in, and if you are in a buyer's or a seller's market among other things. This is when having an experienced realtor will be especially helpful. Along with the offer of how much you are willing to pay for the house, you might want to ask for things like, "keep the drapes," or "fix the broken window," or "seller pays closing costs." Those are some of your negotiations.

Within an agreed-upon timeframe, but usually within twenty-four hours, the owner and their representative will reply to the offer. They can say yes, no, or present a counter offer. Rarely is the first offer accepted outright. This can go back and forth a few times. Again, negotiations are on the table. "Yes, you can keep the drapes, but we don't want to fix the window."

The offer is contingent on a home inspection, paid for by the potential buyer. Your realtor or lender will recommend a professional home inspector and you absolutely don't want to skip this step. The inspector is paid to give a report of every little thing he or she can find that is wrong with the house. Once the full report is presented, the owner may have some things they are required to fix or there may be more negotiations.

> **Don't show your enthusiasm if you love the house. If the owner knows you will buy the house no matter what, that gives you less negotiating power.**

Depending on location, other types of inspections are also required – foundation inspections, termite inspections, well, septic, or radon inspections. It just depends on what kinds of things can be problematic in that particular geographical area.

Once the inspection is done, an appraiser is hired to make sure the property is worth what you're paying. The mortgage lender hires them, but you absorb the cost. Meanwhile, the lender also has a title search done by a title company or an attorney. Once both of those things are done, you'll set a date for the closing.

The closing will usually take a couple of hours. You may bring anyone along with you to the closing. You'll sit at a table with your realtor, the closing attorney, and the seller's realtor or representative. You'll sign a zillion papers, which you'll have to trust are all correct and in order, because there's no way you can read them all. It's a happy occasion and there will be smiles, handshakes, and photos. Once everything is signed, you'll walk away from closing with the keys and rights to the property – and a mortgage!

I hear people say, "I like to stay busy
because it makes the time go faster."
I wonder... What's the hurry?

— Laura Thomae Young

– 14 –

ADULTING WITH YOUR TIME

"Busy or bored, you get twenty-four hours. You get the same amount of time as Bill Gates, Bono, the CEO, the janitor, the airplane pilot, and the kindergarten teacher."

When it comes to time, I'm a linear thinker. I picture the story of my life on a long timeline, a roll of paper stretched out across the room from left to right. On the far left end is birth and childhood. On the far right end is old age and death. I assume that I am somewhere about in the middle of the timeline, and if you're in your twenties, that you are somewhere still toward the left end, slightly to the left of the middle.

(Truth be told, any one of us could be at the far right and not know it, for we absolutely cannot know what tomorrow brings.)

What's the difference between time and money? If you spend money, you can get more. If you spend time, it's gone forever. You can't save it up for later, you can't stockpile it, and you can't go back and have a "do-over." Gone is gone. Minutes turn into days, which turn into years. So spend your time wisely!

Of all the things in your life to take care of, time is the most important. Guard it, use it wisely, don't kill time or waste it. Fill it up to the brim. Squeeze every ounce of every minute! One day, you'll look back and wonder where it all went. Pay attention to your minutes and your hours and your days, and you will be paying attention to your life.

> **What's the difference between time and money? If you spend money, you can get more. If you spend time, it's gone forever.**

Isn't it amazing that regardless of what's going on in your life, you receive the same amount of time every day? Busy or bored, you get twenty-four hours. You get the same amount of time as Bill Gates, Bono, the CEO, the janitor, the airplane pilot, and the kindergarten teacher.

If you're waiting on something wonderful, time moves slowly. If you're up against a deadline, it moves too quickly. In truth, however, we know that a minute equals a minute no matter what. We can't speed up time and we can't slow it down.

We talk of saving time, but we can't save it. A time-saving device means that you will spend less time doing that activity. It doesn't save time, it just allows you to divide your day differently. For example, washing and drying your clothes in a machine, rather than by hand as they did in the olden days, "saves time." However, to wash your clothes by hand meant spending several hours on that project. Nowadays we wash our clothes in a machine. Tossing them in and pulling them out takes only a few minutes. We can then spend our time doing other activities while our machine "spends time" doing the washing.

Time feels faster for me now. From Christmas morning to Christmas morning, a year seemed an eternity when I was a child. Now I feel I've hardly put my Christmas decorations away before it's time to drag them all back out again. My aunt once told me that time feels faster when you get older because it's a smaller percentage of your life. As a ten-year-old, a year is one-tenth of your life. As a forty-year-old, it's only a fortieth.

Making time for it all

Perhaps you have heard the following popular story, which illustrates how important it is to prioritize your time for the important things in your life.

> **In order to say yes to the things that are important to you, you have to say no to other things.**

A teacher places a glass jar on her table in front of her students. "This represents your life," she says. "You can fill it with whatever you desire."

The teacher takes a bag of large rocks and places them one by one into the jar.

"These rocks represent the important things in your life. These are the things that are both important now and will matter later in your life."

When the jar was filled to the top and no more rocks would fit, she asked the class, "Is this jar full?" Everyone in the class said, "Yes."

The teacher then takes out a second bag, this one filled with pebbles. She scoops out several handfuls of pebbles and lets them fall into the jar, shaking the jar slightly so the pebbles fill the spaces between the rocks. "These are the secondary things in your life. Less essential than the big rocks, but still important."

Again she asked the class, "Is this jar full now?" Everyone in the class answered again, "Yes."

The teacher then takes out a small bag of sand. She pours the sand into the jar and gently agitates it until it fills the space between the pebbles.

"Finally," she said, "the sand represents the little stuff – the less important things - in our lives. Playing games, watching TV, or hanging out on social media."

The teacher looks out over the class and asks, "Can you see what would have happened if we started with the sand or the pebbles? We always have to put the big rocks in first."

> *I knew I was really grown up when I had a savings account. I moved to a new city and didn't have one, so learning how to budget and work hard has been Adulting for me.*
>
> --Courtney K., 23

Lastly, the teacher took out a cup of coffee. Into the very full jar, she poured the coffee.

"And no matter how full your life is," she said, "you always have room for a cup of coffee with a friend."

What are your big rocks? Those unchangeable time chunks that are the non-negotiables in your life?

Start by dividing your day into segments. Work and sleep are the biggest chunks of time during the workweek for most of us. Those are the big rocks.

What else needs to be added to that? Commute? Subtract an hour. Showering and getting dressed? Another hour. Preparing (or purchasing) food and eating. Another hour or two.

Once you've whittled down the time, the discretionary time left over is the time you have to fit in everything else. If you are in a traditional Monday-through-Friday job, you'll have the weekends you can also fill with activities.

> **You usually aren't choosing between good and bad. You have to choose between good and better or, harder still, good and good.**

Exercising, relaxing and playing, attending religious services, engaging in hobbies, socializing, working side hustles, shopping, reading, playing or enjoying music, taking a class, doing house and yard work, caring for others, traveling, and on and on the list goes.

How in the world can you fit it all in?

Schedule it

Planning ahead is everything. The old adage, "Fail to plan and you plan to fail," is true. For some reason actually scheduling things on the calendar seems a little silly when you add things like, "Call Mom," or "Go to the gym." However, *not* planning them and not putting them on the calendar can keep those priorities from ever making it into your life.

If you're having trouble fitting everything in that you want, use a paper planner or a schedule on your phone or computer, and be *absolutely ridiculous* about scheduling everything! You may find that the reason you're feeling overwhelmed is that you can't possibly fit everything into your discretionary time!

Try making an entire daily schedule for each thing you want to do or accomplish. How long does it take, for example, to get up, shower and dress, eat breakfast, and get out the door? Can you squeeze in

> **Getting up early has been one of the most valuable things I've implemented to redeem my time.**

more? If you economize, can you get in exercise, a walk, time for sitting quietly and meditating? Do you need to get up earlier for those things to happen?

Prioritize

In order to say yes to the things that are important to you, you have to say no to other things. And here's the difficult part - you usually aren't choosing between good and bad. You have to choose between good and better or, harder still, good and good.

Why is that?

We eliminate from the table all the things we don't want to do or things we know don't matter. Those never even make it into our conscious choices. The things we are left with are the things we need to do, the things we should do, and the things we want to do.

Things we *need* to do and *should* do include tasks like: work, clean, grocery shop, shower and dress, pay bills, care for belongings, etc.

Things we *want* to do are more likely hobbies and social events like: hanging out with friends, Netflix binges, watching or participating in sports, (although participation can count as exercise so it kind of crosses the line between "need" and "want"), and spending time on social media.

Where the most trouble lies is adding things to our schedules that are priorities but not urgencies. These are the things that need to get done, but get neglected because there aren't immediate consequences to putting them off.

If I don't put gas in my car, I will eventually run out on the side of the road. I hate stopping for gas and I hate pumping it. But if I don't do it, there will be immediate consequences.

I don't particularly like going to the gym. I like it once I'm there - I especially like it as I'm leaving - but I have a very hard time *wanting* to go. If I don't go to the gym, my body gets out of shape, flabby, and weak. But not immediately. I don't see immediate results from going to the gym nor do I see immediate results from not going. This kind of habit is one of the hardest things to schedule.

Getting Up Early

Getting up early has been one of the most valuable things I've implemented to redeem my time. I follow Hal Elrod's *Miracle Morning* book – a six-step "perfect morning" plan, which I've personalized a bit to better fit me - and get up early almost every day, even on weekends. I've learned to love early mornings. It's quiet, there's no competition for my time, so I can get up and "do" my morning routine.

The six-tep Miracle Morning consists of Silence, Affirmations, Visualization, Exercise, Reading, and Writing (he calls it Scribing.) I'm a Christian, so my silence and reading centers around Bible reading, prayer, and journaling. I'm usually working on a writing project, and early morning is the best time to get some writing in. Exercise is walking the dog. I love taking him out in the early morning when the neighborhood is quiet. Affirmations have become a part of my life. I say aloud what I believe to be true of me, and then I stretch my goals with visualization.

> **The six-step Miracle Morning consists of:**
> **Silence**
> **Affirmations**
> **Visualization**
> **Exercise**
> **Reading**
> **Writing**

Visualization and affirmations have helped me picture my success and make it real in my mind. As I make big goals, set out to achieve them and work *every day* toward achieving them, I'm able to believe the affirmations I speak aloud. My mouth says them, my ears hear them – in my own voice – and I am able to believe that they are true. The more I have believed them, the more they have become true. I speak them even when I doubt. As I believe them, I begin to live them out – I am making my own reality.

I encourage you to read Hal's book, *The Miracle Morning*, and implement the six steps into your life too. It took me years to see the value in daily quiet time, but now I can't imagine my life without it.

When the pain of staying the same
is greater than the pain of change —
that's when motivation kicks in.

— Laura Thomae Young

– 15 –
Adulting with The Right Habits

"The challenge is actually doing what you know...over and over again. It's not one BIG thing; it's lots of little things."

Now you may ask, "What about all the Hard Things I should *constantly* be doing? Not just the one-off like getting a tire fixed, making my own doctor's appointment, etc. What about things like cooking, keeping up with my finances, being on time, taking care of my car, exercising, laundry, organization, the everyday Adulting things?"

Some things are one-time achievements. Do the Hard Thing, finished, and we're good. Tah-Dah! Adulted! Gold Star!

Adulting Like a Boss

But there are lots of other things in Adulting that take daily constant attention. How come we don't do those things? It's like pulling the all-nighter in college, versus the (better) system of studying diligently all semester.

> **Some people call it ritual. Some call it habit. Some call it routine. However, you slice it, it's the little things you do, day after day, that build into the BIG things.**

The problem is not that you don't know how - anybody can learn how. *The challenge is actually doing what you know...over and over again.*

It's not one BIG thing; it's lots of little things.

Here are a few things you should know about these kinds of habits - the ones you need to succeed at Adulting:
- You'll accomplish less by trying to do it all at once.
- A little at a time goes a long way.
- They're usually a little unpleasant.
- You'll often have to work to fit them into your schedule.

The habits we want to create in our life should be attainable and sustainable. Let me use the example of brushing and flossing your teeth. I would guess that you brush your teeth a couple of times a day at a minimum, right? Brushing – yep. Got it. Daily - 1x, 2x, 3x.

But flossing?

Flossing is something everyone knows they *should* do, but most people don't. Why not? Is it for lack of information? Lack of skill? Lack of belief that it really is a good thing to do? Doubtful.

So why don't most people floss? And I don't mean the mad dash for floss on the day of the dentist appointment, but every day, day after day.

Some people call it *ritual*. Some call it *habit*. Some call it *routine*. However, you slice it, it's the little things you do, day after day, that build into the BIG things. In the example of flossing – the BIG things are healthy teeth and gums.

Instant gratification vs. long-term results

Brush your teeth and you get that fresh feeling in your mouth. It's immediately rewarding. Some habits though, like flossing, only show progress when you do them over and over. When you miss a day, nothing bad happens. So, you figure it doesn't really matter.

> **Some bad habits give me an immediate sense of gratification. And since nothing bad happens, my brain tells me it must be okay. But the consequences are going to be down the road a bit — poor health, low energy, and added pounds. It's cumulative and delayed.**

Let me give you another example.

I eat a few cookies at a party. Nobody judges me. Nothing bad happens. So, I eat a few more. And then a few more. And down down down I go on the slippery slope. I eat cookies because I like them, they taste good, and they give me an immediate sense of gratification. And again, since nothing bad happens, my brain tells me it must be okay.

Now you and I both know that a steady diet of a plateful of cookies is going to be bad for me. We know that the consequences of that bad habit are going to be down the road a bit – poor health, low energy, and added pounds. It's cumulative and delayed.

Now lest you think of me as a cookie-hater, I know a few cookies won't completely sabotage my weeks and weeks of baked chicken and broccoli. But I also know that as I grow older and have to watch my waistline more carefully, saying "yes" to cookies adds up, just as saying "no" to junk food, snacks, and sweets will add up in a positive way.

Okay, no more guilt about eating cookies and not flossing. Let's move on and learn how to build some good habits into your life.

Always learning — READ!!!

A few years ago, my husband was traveling and had a stopover in the Houston airport. As he passed by one of the people-mover carts, he noticed an elderly man looking quite lost as he tried to converse in Spanish with a flustered airport employee. Hoping he could help (he's bilingual), Steve walked over and offered his assistance. Both the employee and the elderly gentleman were visibly relieved to have an interpreter.

The older gentleman was trying to get to his next gate but didn't know where it was or what to do. He was

> I've built up an appetite for more reading — by reading!

trying to get help, but without the language skills or the tenacity to make his desires known, he was helpless. Steve pointed out the direction the man needed and added, "Just look for Gate A. That's where you need to go next."

Sadly, the man hung his head. In Spanish, he told Steve, "I don't know how to read."

> **Reading will change you more than any other activity.**

With high literacy rates in the United States, it's hard for us to imagine what it must be like for people to puzzle over something as simple as the letter "A." Learning to read is a rite of passage for children. It opens up doors like nothing else. Yet somewhere along the way, the magic fades and we take reading for granted.

Practically every community in America has a library – free access to almost any book you can imagine, including e-books and audio books. Amazon has an "all-you-can-read" e-book program for a small monthly fee. If we aren't reading enough, it's not for lack of access!

Reading three books on one subject makes you an expert, according to some. Though, I suppose that would depend on the subject! I don't think I'd be an expert at brain surgery by reading three books, but I'd sure know more about it than the average person.

If you're not much of a reader, I appreciate the fact that you've chosen to read this book. It proves that you can do it!

I encourage you to read! For many years I would sandwich books that are "good for you" between novels, because my interest in fiction would keep my reading momentum going. I didn't particularly enjoy reading non-fiction books, but knew I'd learn a lot. Nowadays, I enjoy non-fiction more than novels. I've built up an appetite for more reading – by reading!

Growing your attention span.

If you have a short attention span and find you can't read for more than a few minutes at a time without losing your train of thought, I have good news - you can grow your attention span by practice.

First, find a book you think you'll be interested in. I suggest getting several books from the library and trying different ones until you find something you can stick with. Fiction or nonfiction doesn't really matter at this point, just get whatever will keep your attention. Get books with pictures, books on hobbies, or books on any subject you're interested in. It doesn't matter what subject or even what reading level.

If you're *really* not a reader, try the juvenile fiction section of the library and get a teen novel. They are written at an easier-to-read level and will be entertaining and fun. Think of this as practicing scales on the piano. You'll get to Beethoven later! The main thing right now is to create a habit.

Next, commit to read just five to ten minutes per day. That's it. Early in the morning, late at night, or on your lunch hour or break – set the timer, and read. Keep a bookmark so you'll know where you last left off, and try not to miss a day for ten days in a row.

After ten days, increase your time to fifteen minutes. Then after fifteen days in a row, stretch it to twenty minutes, and continue the pattern until you find you can read for up to an hour at each sitting.

In his autobiography, *Gifted Hands*, neurosurgeon Ben Carson explains his rise from being a failing student to one of the top students of his class. His mother began requiring that her sons read every day before watching television. She didn't have a requirement for what they were reading, only that they read two books per week and present her with a written report of what they were reading. Feigning poor eyesight, she had her boys read the book reports aloud to her. It wasn't until years later that they discovered she was illiterate!

That one activity – reading – took two failing students from the bottom all the way to the top of their respective classes. She didn't require them to study or do their homework or even scold them about their grades. Just read.

> When I read or hear something amazing that someone else has done, then I am sure I can reach my goals too!

Reading will change you.

Reading will change you more than any other activity. If you want to see positive changes in your life, read. If you want to grow as a person, read. If you want to improve yourself, read. If you want to learn, read.

You should read. You must read.

Think you don't have time to read? Here are a few suggestions for when you can fit it in:
- First thing in the morning
- Late at night
- During your lunch hour
- Instead of watching television

Once you've begun the habit of reading and built the muscle of attention span, begin pushing yourself to read inspirational, motivational, or informational books. You may choose to sandwich in those books between other types of reading material that's fun and effortless, like I did, to create the momentum. By pushing yourself, you'll expand your vocabulary, your knowledge, and your wisdom.

Read.

Listen to and read inspirational & motivational materials

I read an inspirational story a few years ago about Spencer West, a man who has no legs and uses his hands to transport himself. As if that were not enough to inspire, he also took up mountain climbing. The article was about a recent climb he had achieved on Mount Kilimanjaro, one of the world's most difficult mountains to summit. Reading about that terrific feat made me feel like, "Oh my gosh, I'm the laziest person on the planet."

I was inspired and moved. The next day I took up jogging! (In case you're interested, I did the "Couch-to-5K" program. I couldn't run more than a few minutes when I started. It's a great program if you're new to running.)

More recently, my friend's twelve-year-old daughter, Lucy, discovered that her pen pal in Uganda, Africa, didn't have access to clean drinking water. Lucy started a campaign and raised enough money to fly to Uganda and present her pen pal's village leaders with a water filtration system that would give the whole village access to clean drinking water.

Reading stories like Lucy's is rousing to me. She's just a little girl and she's doing all that? What am I doing for others? Lucy's story bumped up my efforts in humanitarianism.

When I read or hear about people like Lucy or Spencer, I am inspired. I am inspired to DO more and TRY more and RISK more. When I read or hear something amazing that someone else has done, then I am sure I can reach my goals too! That's *why* I read and listen to inspirational stories.

Books can transform your mindset, and, as a result, your life. After reading Jen Sincero's book, *You are a Badass*, my mindset tells me that now I, too, am a Badass!

> There's only one me in this world, and no one is uniquely qualified to say or do the things that I am supposed to say and do.

I'm an Old Testament Bible buff, and I love reading and re-reading the stories of the less-than-perfect heroes like the young shepherd boy, David, who fought lions and giants. I love the story of Nehemiah, who rallied his people to rebuild the wall around Jerusalem with threats so imminent that they worked with a tool in one hand and a sword in the other. And then there's Moses, who appealed to the Egyptian Pharaoh to free what was probably a million Israelite slaves, but had his brother do the talking because Moses had a speech impediment.

You see, it takes a steady diet of stories for me to *stay* inspired. Hearing how others have overcome adversity, worked hard to reach a goal, or stayed the course when everything seemed to be against them makes me believe I can do the same.

I don't want to go through life living in mediocrity. I've had plenty of seasons of that and I find it to be boring and meaningless. I want to do more and be more. I want to go to bed each night tired because I've used up all my energy. I want to wake up excited about what I get to do that day. I want to be in love with life and never ever wish my days away. I want to stretch myself and become the best version of me.

There's only one me in this world, and no one is uniquely qualified to say or do the things that I am supposed to say and do.

The same goes for you. No one else has your same story. You are uniquely gifted at being YOU. So be the very best YOU that you can be. And yes, that's hard. It's easy to get into a rut of "day in and day out" and settle for ho-hum. But that's no way to live! Stretch for goals you're not sure you can reach. Read. Listen to people who are smarter than you, who inspire you, who make you believe in yourself.

Play outside

Why do I include the act of going outside in a book on Adulting?

As I have interviewed dozens of young millennial women, I have found that a common theme is that they suffer from anxiety and stress. Living in the 21st century, everything about anything is broadcasted on the news, so there's the whole world to worry about. On the personal level, though, finances, student debt, jobs – all these add up and can overwhelm with a feeling of frustration, fear, and anxiety.

You can't make all that just simply go away by playing outside, but there is a real power in the threefold combination of being in unadulterated natural surroundings, absorbing serotonin-producing sunlight, and *play*. As adults, we shouldn't lose our sense of play, nor should we underestimate the power of nature to de-stress our lives. Ingesting the beauty and majesty of nature along with the added benefits of exercise and sunshine naturally elevates our mood.

When I was growing up in Louisiana, my mom insisted that we go outside and play. Every day. We had outdoor toys – swing set, see-saw, even a zip line was set up to go from tree to tree. I climbed trees, rode horses, rode my bike, played basketball in the driveway, played in our barn, played touch football with my sisters and the neighbor kids, played with our cats and dogs, and played in the water sprinkler.

> **As adults, we shouldn't lose our sense of play, nor should we underestimate the power of nature to de-stress our lives.**

It wasn't all play though; we also worked outdoors. We picked blackberries in the summer and harvested pecans in the winter. We cut

Adulting Like a Boss

the grass, hoed the garden, put out hay for the cows, and did other outdoor chores. I was outdoors practically all the time as a child.

Fast forward to my life today, and I spend the majority of my Mondays through Fridays indoors in climate-controlled carpeted buildings. I get outdoors whenever I can, but most of the time, I'm inside. I didn't think twice about being outdoors as a kid, and now it's both an effort and a special pleasure to get outside. My house has a big deck across the back, and I spend as much time out there as possible. The office space I occupy has a patio with tables and chairs, so I often eat lunch outdoors. Rarely, though, are my hands in dirt or my toes in the grass. I enjoy hiking, so I make an effort to take short hikes during the summer when the daylight hours are longer and I can get in a short walk before dark.

Being in touch with nature is therapeutic, and the Japanese practice of getting outdoors for a hike in the woods, called "forest bathing," is catching on in the United States. Getting out and enjoying trees and grass and sunshine is good for the body and good for the soul. For those of us chained to the indoors, it is especially therapeutic and important for our wellbeing.

> **Being outdoors reduces stress. Nature soothes the soul. Fresh air is good for you.**

When you get to choose, choose to be outdoors. Swim in the lake instead of the pool. Grab a blanket and take a picnic lunch to the park. Go camping. Go to the mountains or the beach if you can. Get involved in community sports or support a local little league team by sitting in the bleachers and cheering them on. Volunteer in beautification projects or community gardens.

Being outdoors reduces stress. Nature soothes the soul. Fresh air is good for you. Sitting on a beach and contemplating the vastness of the ocean, or being amazed by the monstrosity of a mountain are great for helping you get into the right perspective on life's problems and challenges.

If you want to have clearer thinking and a better grasp on life, go outside with your body in motion. Enjoy nature. Be one with the earth. Get dirt under your fingernails and wriggle your toes in the grass or mud. However you want to put it, bring out the kid in you and play outside.

Build the Habit of Being on Time

My grandpa, in his later years, drove one speed – thirty miles per hour. It didn't matter where he was – on the highway or out in the fields of our farm. We'd urge him to speed up on the highways, as a long line of cars would pile up behind us.

"Nope," he'd say. "If you want to get there sooner, leave earlier!"

Being on time for work, social events, family dinners, even coffee dates with friends – this habit shows respect for others. It shows that you respect the fact that they are busy and lead full, productive lives. And if that's true, then the opposite is also true – being *late* for work, social events, family dinners, and coffee dates with friends shows DISrespect.

Being late basically says to others, "I don't know what you people are doing with your day, but I am busy and important. You'll just need to wait on me."

Of course, everybody has circumstances that delay them – unexpected traffic delays, a flat tire, forgetting your keys and consequently locking yourself out of your house or apartment (hmmm.. wonder why I thought of that one!), but being consistently on time (even early!!!) is Hard – and a very Adulty thing to do.

Think of the last time you were left waiting on someone who was late. It was probably annoying and you may have felt disrespected.

We can do little tricks to make ourselves be on time, like setting our clocks ahead. But that doesn't really work because we know we're tricking ourselves. We catch on to our own little tricks!

> **Think of the last time you were left waiting on someone who was late. It was probably annoying and you may have felt disrespected.**

If you're constantly late, first figure out what's making you late. Reverse engineer it. The last few times you were late, what was the real reason? Work on fixing ONE thing that addresses the issue. Here are a few common reasons people are often late and solutions for conquering them:

- **Sleeping in** – Are you sleeping in too late? Are you just too sleepy to get up? The solution starts with an earlier bedtime. And if the alarm doesn't wake you, or you hit the snooze a half-dozen times, consider putting the alarm clock (or phone) across the room.
- **Packed schedule** – Are you trying to fit too much into your schedule? Are you over-estimating what you are actually able to accomplish in one day? Consider curbing your schedule to be more realistic.

- **Unprepared** – Think through what you'll need in order to leave on time. Many times tardiness is due to looking for the keys or grabbing one more thing before you head out the door. Get everything you'll need and have it by the door ahead of time. For example, pack your lunch the night before and have it in the fridge, ready to go.
- **Frivolous decision-making** – Deciding what to wear is a common source of lateness. Have your clothes planned and ready to go the day before. If you're a constant last-minute-change-your-mind'er, have a backup outfit planned as well.
- **Traffic** – Underestimating the commute time can make you late. Driving fast doesn't help! It will only make you more late (and frustrated) if you get a speeding ticket! Leave fifteen or twenty minutes earlier than needed to account for excessive traffic. Then if you get there early, have a book ready and read a few minutes.

Figure out what the delay is, and see how you can ADULT your way out of it!

HOW TO...

Take Care of Your Car

This is definitely not an exhaustive list of caring for your car, but here are the basics that you need to be doing:

- **Keep your car clean and waxed** – Some **substances** like bird poo or salt (from winter salted roads) will damage the finish of your car if not washed off in a timely manner.
- **Check your headlights and blinkers** – A fast blinker means a blinker bulb is out. They're usually fairly simple to replace, and you can get a replacement at any auto parts store. Don't buy the cheap-o version of the replacement bulbs – they don't last.
- **Check your oil and change it every 5,000 miles** – Ask whoever changes your oil to check the air filter too. With each oil change, you should have your oil filter changed. It's easy to check your oil yourself and add it if you're low, but you need special tools to change your oil. There are lots of places that do it very inexpensively (around $30-$40) and can do it while you wait. It only takes about 30 minutes.
- **Make sure you have antifreeze** - In the winter it will keep the water (that cools your engine) from freezing and locking the engine. Most oil-change places will check all of your car's fluids when you get the oil changed.
- **Check your tire pressure** – Rotate and/or replace your tires as needed. Driving on bad tires is dangerous. Don't compromise your safety. While you can't prevent all flat tires, keeping your tires in good shape will help. If you get a flat from a puncture, such as a nail, many times it can be fixed and the tire doesn't have to be replaced.

- **Keep your windshield wiper fluid filled** – it's easy to fill yourself. Look under the hood or check the manual and make sure you put the right fluids into the right recipients! Washer fluid can be found at any gas station, convenience store, or an auto parts store.
- **Pay attention to warning lights, gauges, or funny sounds your car makes** – Get it checked immediately. Ignoring a warning light, gauge, or sound can turn a **small** problem into a much bigger one, including total destruction of your engine.
- **Pay attention to anything that is leaking from your car** – Get it checked immediately. No fluid is supposed to leak from your car except condensation from your air conditioner. If there is any dark-colored or green-colored fluid dripping out, get it checked immediately.
- **Change your brake pads** – A persistent squeak when you **stop** means they need to be replaced. A tire place, brake place, or even your regular mechanic can check and replace your pads.
- **Ask friends and family for a reliable and trustworthy mechanic** – And let the mechanic know who sent you. You don't want someone to take advantage of you if you don't know much about cars. Your best bet is to have a personal connection. If not, check out reviews online before trusting a mechanic.

Integrity is doing the right thing when no one is looking. Always, even when you're alone, do the right thing.

— Laura Thomae Young

– 16 –

ADULTING OVER AND OVER

"One of the positive things about deciding and implementing a new habit is that you have already made a firm decision. You don't have to decide if you're going to do it. That's been done. Now you just have to act."

Nothing will help you more in life like building good habits. Once you have a good habit in place, you don't even have to think about it. It becomes second nature, a part of your life. It's not work anymore. You do it without even thinking. You can't imagine living without doing it.

But it's a process to get there. It doesn't happen overnight, and the common belief that six weeks is all it takes to build a good habit may or may not hold true – depending on how big the change is, and how committed you are.

There are five steps to getting there that everyone has to go through.

Step 1 – Know this – the beginning is going to be excruciatingly painful

If you're trying to build a new habit, a million reasons (ahem, excuses) will begin to raise their ugly heads.

"I don't know how." "I don't have the right tools." "It's too hard."

Building a new habit into your life – like cooking instead of eating out, hanging up your keys instead of tossing them wherever, keeping up with your budget instead of not paying attention – is going to be painful. You'll get it wrong sometimes. You'll slip back into old habits. But you CAN change almost anything in your life!

Oftentimes, the bigger the habit, the more difficult to make the transformation. Cooking or hanging up keys is one thing. Creating a habit of healthy relationships is quite another. Yet for almost any life habit, there are a few principles that will help you get to where you want to go.

When the pain of staying the same is greater than the pain of change, that's when we make a transformation.

Think of this stage as pulling a thorn out of your foot – it has to happen. Letting a thorn stay in your foot will be worse in the long run, but oftentimes, it hurts like heck to pull it out. The pain of keeping the thorn in your foot, though, is worse than the pain of pulling it out.

Likewise, *when the pain of staying the same is greater than the pain of change, that's when we take a look at our lives and make a transformation.*

There are a few ways you can make this stage a little less painful.

Engage a partner.

Getting a buddy to do it with you is great motivation. There is power in accountability. Knowing that someone is meeting up with you at the gym is a good reason not to miss a session. Booking sessions with a coach, taking a class, having someone who expects you to show up – those are all gold.

> Even nature teaches us that wonderful things can happen by a small, seemingly insignificant action taking place, little by little over time.

If your new habit is not partner-friendly, consider engaging a partner just for accountability. Ask them to check on you and give them a report on how you're doing. You've gotta get someone on board who won't take your crap and let you off the hook.

Environmental engineering.

Creating a space that makes it difficult to fail and easy to succeed has more power than you can imagine. Things like getting the sugar out of the house if you are watching your weight. Or having your gym clothes on the foot of the bed to put on first thing in the morning (or even sleeping in them!). Have healthy snacks sitting out on the table, and hide the sweets. Put the television remote in the closet and a book by your favorite chair. Engineer your environment so that the *right* choice is the *easy* choice. It's one less hurdle you'll have to cross.

Visual reminders and rewards.

Make a chart and give yourself a gold star, put an app on your phone that tracks your progress, put a note on your bathroom mirror – do whatever works for you as a visual reminder of the habit you are trying to change and a big ol' checkmark when you accomplish your goal. It's amazing how rewarding it can be to have ten checkmarks in a row for ten days of accomplishing your newfound habit!

Remember, there are two types of habits.

They are the ones that you already know how to do but just don't do, and the ones that you have to learn.

Hanging up your keys, for example, is one you don't have to learn how to do. The hardest part of preparation for this might be putting a nail by the door.

For others habits, like cooking, budgeting or cultivating healthy relationships, you're going to be on a learning curve. For these new, unfamiliar habits, you'll go through several stages before you become proficient.

- **Stage 1 – Learning:** You don't know how to do something so you have to learn. You research, read, ask everyone you know, watch how-to videos. YouTube becomes your best friend. It's easy to get stuck at this stage, by the way. If you're a lover of learning, you can park here and never get to Stage 2, using research and learning as an excuse not to take action.

- **Stage 2 – Implementation:** You take action on the new habit, but you're uncomfortable. It still doesn't feel quite natural. You're still learning, but now you're learning as you take action. You discover better or more efficient ways to do this habit. (An example of this is if you are learning to shop, plan, and prepare meals. You might learn that you can order your groceries online and pick them up rather than doing all the shopping in person.)

- **Stage 3 – Awkward traction:** You're still feeling dorky, but you're doing it. The new habit is beginning to take hold in your life. You wonder what other people think, and then you stop caring what people think and realize nobody was thinking about you at all. You're fairly confident now. (An example is walking into the gym and going straight to the treadmill, rather than wandering around wondering what to do next.)

- **Stage 4 – You're the boss:** You know exactly what to do and are encouraging others to join in. For example, you can make menus and execute them perfectly. Or you graduate from a nail to a cute key hook by the back door and remember to hang your keys. You're trying to build a quiet-time morning habit, and you graduate from a notebook to a leather journal. You are now confident in the *How-To*.

Step 2 – You're past the pain and now it's just difficult

After a few weeks of a new habit, you'll still find it difficult to implement regularly. You've learned how to do it. You've been doing the new habit - some of the time. But it still feels unnatural and you really don't WANT to. You're having to force yourself because you'd really rather just do the easy thing. You're sick and tired of it and wish you could just forget about it. But you keep going….

One of the positive things about deciding and implementing a new habit, though, is that you have already made a firm decision. You don't have to *decide* if you're going to do it. That's been done. Now you just have to *act*.

Step 3 — Ugh, this is hard....

Okay, you've got this. It's not so painful anymore, but it still takes a tremendous amount of effort. You still may not WANT to do it, but at this point, you've played out all your arguments in your head, and they don't really fly with you anymore.

> Grit, the tenacity to keep on keepin' on, is the one predictor in a person's life that will likely result in success.

This is a stage where it's really easy to quit, because the newness has worn off and the thrill is gone. But keep going! The good part is coming.

Step 4 — Habit

Now that you've been doing this for some time, you do it without thinking. You realize you don't even have to make an effort, it just comes naturally. You floss. You do a daily check on your bank balance. You hang up your keys. You stop by the grocery instead of the fast food restaurant. You've arrived. This is better! Life is better. And now we get to the final step!

Step 5 — Can't imagine life without it!

Now you're Adulting Like a Boss in this area of your life. You pass the fast food restaurant and roll your eyes. You say to yourself, "Oh, I can't believe all those people are eating that nasty fast food." You pack for your trip to Europe that you've saved for. Your dental hygienist asks you to give a class on flossing. You hang up your keys without even thinking about it – to the point where you ask yourself, "What did I do with my keys?" and you see that you hung them up. You hear angels singing. Well, okay, maybe we're going too far here, but you get the picture.

How long it takes in each step depends on what the habit is, how many times you fall off the wagon in the process, and how motivated you are to change. A habit like hanging your keys up can take a few weeks to form. A habit like engaging in healthy relationships may take years.

Either way, you're on the right path to Adulting Like a Boss.

Doing it over and over

I've been spelunking a few times. Spelunking is you and a few friends, a Saturday afternoon, flashlight in hand, exploring a cave on your hands and knees. Not to be confused with caving, as my friend Phillip pointed out. Phillip, a serious caving guide, cringes at the word "spelunking" for what he does. Caving is a planned trip with a guide and a map. You carry things like rope, helmets, and special equipment. Caving is serious business, and the best description I have heard is, "Cavers are the ones who rescue spelunkers!"

> **We overestimate what we can do in one year and underestimate what we can do in two years.**

A couple hours' drive from my home in Nashville is a place called Ruby Falls. It's a huge cavern that was opened up to the public about a hundred years ago. Someone had the genius idea that people would pay to tour the cavern if there was easy access. In the last hundred years, thousands of visitors have taken the elevator down into the cave and walked down the developed pathways, complete with handrails and colored lights that highlight the natural beauty of the waterfalls deep down in the earth.

I'm not sure that kind of experience would fall into the category of caving or spelunking – probably neither! Either way, if you've ever had the experience of spelunking, caving, or "tourist walking" through a cave, one of the amazing experiences is seeing the stalactites and stalagmites.

Stalactites are the long, pointed rocks that hang from the ceiling of the cave, formed over hundreds of thousands of years by a steady drip drip drip of water that carries with it minerals and sand, until a rock formation is formed. Stalagmites are their opposite. They jut up from the cave floor, formed from the drip drip drip onto the cave floor. (I remember the difference because stalactites "hold tight" from the ceiling.)

> **You'll slip back into old habits. But you CAN change almost anything in your life!**

We also know this wonder in the story of the Grand Canyon, formed by a single river that flowed and washed away the terrain over many many years. Even the story of the oyster's pearl, formed over time by the secretions of the oyster because of the irritant of a grain of sand, reminds us that beauty is formed over time.

What's my point with this mini science lesson? Even nature teaches us that wonderful things can happen by a small, seemingly insignificant action taking place, little by little over time.

Notice the stalactite hanging from the ceiling is almost joined with the stalagmite rising from the cave's floor.

It's not the BIG things that make our lives different – for better or worse. Rather, major changes come from forming daily habits and rituals that we do over and over again, day after day. Just as brushing and flossing do no significant good if done only the day before we go to the dentist. Oftentimes one BIG thing is not nearly as impactful in our lives as doing the small thing – which may feel at first like the Hard Thing – every day whether we feel like it or not.

Do the Hard Thing – over and over – and it gets easier. But sometimes it's still hard.

Whether you are bucking for a promotion at work, trying to form relationships, or even forming new healthy habits (or ridding yourself of bad ones), keep at it! Work at it every day and give it time. Grit, the tenacity to keep on keepin' on, is the one predictor in a person's life that will likely result in success. Giving up too soon – or becoming discouraged when we don't see immediate results from a few half-hearted efforts done sporadically for a few weeks – is a poor indicator of your power to change. Give it time and give it all you've got.

We overestimate what we can do in one year and underestimate what we can do in two years.

HOW TO...

Do Your Laundry Without Ruining All Your Clothes!

A few tips before you start:

- Buy a brand-name ***laundry detergent***, (Tide, Cheer, All, etc.). Store brands or off-brands may be lower quality. Follow the instructions on the bottle. (I like liquid detergent best.)
- You don't need ***fabric softener*** unless you live in a place with "hard" water. You do need ***stain remover***. I like ***dryer sheets***, but if you choose to use them, get a name brand like Bounce or Snuggle.
- If the tag says "Dry Clean Only," then take the item to the dry cleaner's. Don't try to do it yourself.
- Buy several zipper fabric bags for delicates. These bags are also great for clothing that might snag or pick other clothes or items that can *be* snagged or picked easily. Hand-wash lacy things and bras, or wash them on the delicate cycle in a fabric bag.
- Either completely button or completely unbutton clothing before laundering. Zip up any zippers to prevent them from snagging other clothes.
- Pre-treat stains by following instructions on your stain remover.

Separate your clothes into the following types:

- Heavy clothes, like sweatshirts and jeans
- Lights: pastels, pinks, yellows, etc.
- Darks: reds, blacks, dark green, brown, etc.
- Whites
- Delicates: undies, lacy things, tights or stockings. Use zippered laundry bags for anything with hooks or other closers that could snag or pick, or anything that can get tangled (like tights or long socks).

Most machines will have two setting options – one for water temperature and and one for the cycle type.

- **Water Temperature:** Choose cold/cold (wash and rinse water will both be cold) for most loads. Warm/cold is best for sheets and towels. I don't use hot for anything.
- **Cycle Type:** You may want to use "Permanent Press" for clothing that are not jeans or undies. Choose "Delicates" for your delicate clothes. If in doubt, choose "Normal."

If you are using a top-load washer, start the water and add the detergent. Let the water fill a few inches before adding clothes.

Add clothes to the washer, but don't overstuff. The clothes need room to swish around in the water.

When the cycle is complete, move clothes over to the dryer along with a dryer sheet (if you wish).

ALERT ALERT ALERT!!! Check the lint trap on the dryer and clean it before starting *every* cycle. It's important for the dryer to work efficiently. Plus a clogged lint trap can cause a fire. ***Yes, Really.***

Most dryers will have timed cycles (which is fine for most clothes) or the Perm-Press option. Check clothes after 20-30 minutes. Don't overdry.

Remove the clothes immediately, then shake them out and either hang or fold them right away to prevent wrinkles. Unless you're into ironing or wearing wrinkly clothes. Then leave them wadded up in the basket a few days. That's also cool.

Seek out people whose character and integrity you admire, and befriend them.

— Laura Thomae Young

– 17 –

ADULTING FOR BUILDING NEW FRIENDSHIPS

"Where are the good people? They're likely out doing things — volunteering, getting involved in their community, hanging out in fun places. Find them! And join in."

When it comes to making new friends and finding romance, Adulting couldn't be more challenging. It's so different from college life where you're in proximity with hundreds of other people who are your age and in the same stage of life as you. Ready-made friends are right there! Your roommates, classmates, all the people in your extra-curricular activities - they're everywhere! And if you were lucky in college, you had more than one group of friends. You could choose who to do what with. Likely

Adulting Like a Boss

I knew I was really grown-up when I had to go grocery shopping to fill the empty refrigerator of my first apartment. Food was always something that was just there, like water, in my mom's house. Before I moved out, I had no true realization of how much food costs. I knew it was something that had to be purchased of course, but the reality of how so little could amount to so much money hit me like a freight train.

--Elizabeth C., 21

the biggest problems you had with friends was which activity to choose and who to hang out with on any given night.

As an Adult, you must be both creative and deliberate to find friends. It often doesn't happen organically once you're out of school. If you're fortunate, you'll make friends at work, but oftentimes, the pickings are slim. You'll have to get out of your comfort zone and DO the HARD THING!

Doing the easy thing. Staying home and watching movies alone – will result in the Hard Thing: loneliness.

Doing the Hard Thing. Being proactive and *making* yourself meet people – will result in the easy thing: FRIENDS!

If you are in a small town, if you're shy, or have other challenging factors, it may be harder, but believe me when I tell you that there are other people out there wanting the same thing as you: friends!

So, where do you find these people? Here are a few suggestions:

Family.

Yep, how about sis? Maybe you fought like cats and dogs growing up, but now's the time to cultivate that relationship if she's nearby. There's nothing richer than a friendship with family members.

Volunteering.

Find out what kinds of opportunities are available in your community for volunteering. A pet shelter? Homeless shelter? Soup kitchen? Beautification or restoration group? You'll not only do a good deed, but will also meet other community-minded individuals you'll likely have something in common with.

Community activities.

In the city where I live there are meetups that invite community members to come and meet with like-minded people. Hiking groups, sports groups, writing groups, the list goes on and on. There are also groups advertised that, for a fee, you can meet other single people and go on trips, day activities, or meet for dinner.

On-line group members to meet in person.

If you're in an online group, see if there are any group members in your area, and plan a time to meet up in a coffee shop. If you're leery of meeting strangers, meet during the day at a public space.

Church.
Many churches and other religious organizations will offer activities for single people or for the general populous. Don't be afraid to join in

> Believe me when I tell you that there are other people out there wanting the same thing as you: friends!

the activities in order to get to know people, even if attending church is not your thing. It's likely that you'll meet some very nice people. Be sure and join in the activities – classes, small groups, discussions, festivals, etc., because you're unlikely to make connections if you're just attending a group service. There are often opportunities for volunteering through churches as well.

Take a class.
Seek out adult education or community classes that seem interesting to you and sign up! Going to a class week after week is a sure way to get to know new people. Language classes, art classes, music classes, exercise classes, financial classes, or learn something new like becoming a realtor or CPA. If you find it mildly interesting, sign up!

Where are the good people? They're likely out doing things – volunteering, getting involved in their community, hanging out in fun places. Find them! And join in.

And just a note: You'll likely NOT find them in bars. Don't resort to hanging out alone in a bar hoping to find McDreamy. He's not there. Mr. Creepy is there, and Mr. User is sitting right next to him.

Not knowing how to do something is never a very good excuse not to do it. Everything you need to know is a Google search
or a YouTube video away.

— Laura Thomae Young

– 18 –

ADULTING TO BEAT YOUR EXCUSES

"Don't be afraid of doing the wrong thing.
Be afraid of doing nothing."

So, why don't we do the hard thing? I mean, really, why not? What's holding you back from doing the hard and responsible thing?

Here are a few common excuses and how to overcome them.

It's not just hard – it's too hard!
Sit down with a piece of paper and write out the Hard Thing (or *Things*, but start with one) that you are avoiding. Break it down into steps. What's hard about it? Is it *all* hard or is just one thing about it hard?

What would make it easier? And what would be the benefits if you did it anyway?

Draw a line down the middle of the paper. On the left side, write out what is too hard about doing this thing. On the right side, write ten reasons you have the ability, resources, and brains to overcome it.

Any action we do or don't do is for a reason. Most of us are listening to the radio station WII-FM. *What's In It For Me?* We get something out of everything we do – and *don't* do. Our brains tell us not to change. Our brains try to get everything to stay predictable. The "What's In It For Me" is often comfort. It's more comfortable to stay the same, even when it's that sameness that is holding us back.

Outsmart your brain. Make the change.

Excuse #1: I don't know how

Books, Google, YouTube videos, friends, family. Need I say more?

> It's more comfortable to stay the same, even when it's that sameness that is holding us back.

I swear I think you can learn how to do brain surgery on YouTube. And a library card can give you access to more books, videos, articles, lectures, events, and classes than you could possibly digest in a lifetime.

Not knowing how is a lame excuse. On the easy side of the gamut, learn it on YouTube. On the challenging side, take a course or a class – community colleges, online classes, webinars. In any subject, there are experts who are willing to teach you.

My husband and I decided to begin an online business. There are lots of paid courses, into the thousands of dollars, but we didn't have that kind of cash to spend. We hunted down all the free things – online classes, webinars, seminars, local meetups, and workshops, and found more information than we could possibly take in.

If you really want to know how to do something, the information is out there.

Excuse #2: I don't have the right tools

We have a saying in our house:

"How do things get broken?"

"By using them in a way that you're not supposed to."

Think about it. Using a shoe to drive a nail (done it!) will likely break your shoe. Using a knife as a screwdriver (also done it) will likely break the knife. Using a chair as a ladder – yikes, the danger and the possibility of breaking something other than the chair....

When it comes to driving a nail, I want a hammer. If I need to screw something in, I want a screwdriver (no, not the kind with vodka and orange juice – I may want that kind too but that's NOT what I'm talking about). And if I need to reach something up high, I use a stepstool.

Having and using the right tool is important. Fixing something or completing a task without the right tools just makes it harder for yourself.

So if you have a Hard Thing that you aren't doing, is it because you don't have the right tools?

Let's use budget as an example.

Day 1: You tell yourself, "I must make a budget." And after that it gets fuzzy. "I should probably write something down," you think to yourself. So you go look for a notebook. You finally find a notebook in your old college things. And look, what else is in that pile of things… your yearbook! And now you're lost going down memory lane. So you don't do the budget today. You need a new notebook. You'll wait until you have a chance to get to the store.

Day 2: After spending $36 at the office supply store, you come home with a new notebook, a new mouse and mousepad for your computer, and some decorative stamps they had in the sale bin at the front of the store. So now, you'll get down to business. But wouldn't it be cute to decorate the new notebook with the new stamps? So you spend the next hour and a half making this the cutest notebook you've ever seen.

Day 3: The budget still isn't made. These were not the right tools. Tackling something like making a budget without the right tools can be hard. And hard is what we're learning here, so let's go about it a different way.

For a budget, you need a system. Go to the website and download our free budget sheet at www.adultinglikeaboss.net/freebies. Or someone else's. There are tons of them out there. There are also plenty of online courses you can take to get started. You might just need some software like Quicken. You'll need to have all your financial information handy when you start.

> **Having and using the right tool is important. Fixing something or completing a task without the right tools just makes it harder for yourself.**

With the right tools and the know-how, gathered by scouring the internet, you'll make a lot more progress than jotting down your finances in the back of your half-empty psychology notebook from college.

Excuse #3: I don't have time/energy

Time.

You have 24 hours every day. If you spend 8 hours sleeping, that leaves you 16. Another 8-10 at work, and now we're down to 6 hours.

What is the Hard Thing that others seem to find time to do, but you don't? How much time does it really take?

Can you break it down into small steps where you can do one step each day until it is done?

Is it something that would really only take a few minutes? An hour?

Energy.

Here's the surprising thing about energy: Something in motion stays in motion. It takes a lot more energy to START doing something than it does to KEEP doing it. Even Newton's Law applies here!

Newton's First Law of Motion (simplified)

If an object is not moving, it will not start moving by itself.

*If an object is moving,
it will not stop or change direction unless something pushes it.*

So take a deep breath, start it, and keep at it until it's done. I heard someone speaking recently that she counts down from five, and then jumps up like a rocketship to get her day started. 5…4…3…2…1 and I'm OFF to the races!

> Taking action always beats indecision paralysis.

Excuse #4: Is this the right thing to do?

I just don't know. I don't know if this is even the right thing to do. Maybe I should research a little more. What if this is the wrong thing?

Do you second-guess your actions? Do you find yourself waffling on every decision?

Let's kick this excuse out the door! Taking action always beats indecision paralysis.

If it turns out that you're not going in the right direction, that's okay! A ship that's moving is much easier to steer than one sitting at the dock. Cliché, I know, but it's a great word picture of our own predicament of sitting in inactivity rather than moving forward.

Don't be afraid of doing the wrong thing. Be afraid of doing nothing.

Action trumps ideas! Just DO something already. Quit thinking and planning it to death. The thing about doing Hard Things is that we usually don't WANT to do them. Tackle it. Do it. Action is hard, but it is so much better than regret over having done nothing at all.

Remember that it's the Hard Thing we're trying to do here - the Adulting thing.

Motivation

Here's the thing about taking responsibility and doing the Hard Thing: It's totally worth it.

My kids moan and roll their eyes when I say it, but it's true. "Just do it. And then it will be done!"

> **Action is hard, but it is so much better than regret over having done nothing at all.**

The feeling of satisfaction is so great once you've tackled the Hard Thing. A job well done. Accomplishment. Adulting.

My friend and coworker Lindsey had a flat on the way home from an eight-hour trip. It turned what would normally be a three-hour drive into five, since she had to drive the last leg of the trip on the "donut" tire, which requires you to drive slower, by the way. When she came into the office the next day, she was clearly exhausted. She told me what had happened. And her plan.

"I'm really tired," she said. "I think I'll just see about the tire tomorrow instead of today after work."

When I questioned her about why she was waiting until tomorrow, the truth was that it wasn't fatigue. It was because she didn't know what to do, where to go, or how much it was going to cost.

She had already heard a presentation I'd made on "Doing the Hard Thing" for an Adulting Like a Boss party I'd had at my house. I encouraged her to go ahead and at least make a few phone calls to find out details about replacing the tire.

After ten minutes, the whole process seemed to uncomplicate itself. There was a place on the way home. They had the tire. It wasn't nearly as expensive as she thought, and the whole thing would take less than an hour.

The next day she came into work and I asked her about it. "Yep," she replied, "All taken care of! See! I Adulted!"

As was the case with Lindsey's tire, the Hard Thing you don't want to do is probably NOT as hard as you think. A phone call or two, a YouTube video on "how to," or just asking someone – and usually you can get the Hard Thing done in no time.

Just do it, and then it will be done!

HOW TO...

Check Your Car's Tire Pressure (So you're not driving around on a flat tire!)

What you'll need:

* A tire pressure gauge
* An air compressor

Many gas stations have a coin-fed air compressor with a built-in digital gauge.

You can also buy a manual gauge anywhere auto parts are sold – even most convenience stores and gas stations will have them. They typically only cost a few dollars.

First, find out what your tire pressure should be.

Open the driver's side door, and look in the door jamb. There should be a sticker that has the recommended tire pressure. If you don't see one, check the owner's manual. For some cars, the front and rear tires have different pressure recommendations.

Remove the valve cap from the tire's valve. (Don't lose it!) Push the pressure gauge on hard and fast to get an accurate reading. If you hear air hissing, the gauge is not on the valve correctly – try again. A digital gauge will show the air pressure on the gauge. A manual gauge will pop out a small bar with etched measurements that shows the pressure.

*If your tire's valve cap is green, the tire is filled with nitrogen. Ask your car dealer or local mechanic to find nitrogen fill stations or use this website to find a nitrogen dealer: http://www.getnitrogen.org/

If your tires are low

Following the directions on the air compressor, fill any tires that are low. Recheck the pressure *every 10 seconds.* Be careful not to overfill. There are videos on Youtube of tires exploding from overfilling. Don't be on Youtube.

If you accidentally overfill your tire, let some of the air out by putting the gauge on gently until you hear hissing.

Just do it and it will be done.

— Steve Young (my hubby)

Conclusion

"It's the easy things that make life hard – Do the Hard Thing."

If doing the Hard Thing in life is what makes life easy, then the opposite is also true. Taking the easy path – the one with no resistance – can make life hard for you down the road.

Doing the easy thing seems like a good option when you've worked all day and you just want to come home, hit the couch, and turn on Netflix.

To ignore the warning light on the dash is easier. Do the Hard Thing. Get it checked out at the mechanic.

To run through the drive-through is easier. Do the Hard Thing. Eat your veggies.

Making a budget is hard. Sticking to it is harder. It's easier to spend and not keep up with the balance. Do the Hard Thing with your money. You'll reap the rewards of a budget, a savings account, an emergency fund, and travel money. No surprise declines when you swipe your card. That's the good part that comes after you do the Hard Thing.

> **We don't always see the "down-the-road" consequences of poor choices, procrastination, or inaction, but there are consequences.**

Let me tell you a story about a horseshoe. It's from a famous poem from years ago that has been retold many times through the years. Unless you're a horse person, it may not make sense, so let me give some context.

Horses need shoes. Not tennis shoes or leather shoes, but metal horseshoes. Not all, but most horses that are ridden, especially if they are ridden anywhere other than the grassy greens, need shoes.

A horseshoe is something you've likely seen. It's a U-shaped metal object that is attached to a horse's hard hoof by nails. Someone skilled, called a farrier, with special nails and a certain type of hammer, nails these things to the bottom of a horse's hoof. (Don't worry, it's not cruel and it doesn't hurt the horse.)

Sometimes, a nail can come loose. The horseshoe gets loose as a result, and needs to be tended to, or the horse won't be able to walk or run right. It has to be either repaired or the entire shoe has to be removed and the horse re-shod. The longer you wait to see about repairing it, the worse it's going to get.

So, about that story...

Conclusion

A rider has somewhere important to go – to a battle. And he sees that the horse is in need of a nail for the horseshoe. But either there's no farrier available, or he just doesn't take the time to get it fixed.

Because the nail is loose, the shoe eventually comes off. And because the shoe comes off, the horse is not able to keep up.

Because the horse is not able to keep up, the horse and the rider are unable to go into the battle.

Because this particular rider was a key player in the battle, the battle is lost.

This particular battle was key in the war, and the war is lost, and the kingdom falls into the hands of the enemy.

All because of a nail.

Here's the poem:

> *For want of a nail, the shoe was lost.*
> *For want of a shoe, the horse was lost.*
> *For want of a horse, the rider was lost.*
> *For want of a rider, the battle was lost.*
> *For want of a battle, the kingdom was lost,*
> *And all for the want of a horseshoe nail.*

We don't always see the "down-the-road" consequences of poor choices, procrastination, or inaction, but there *are* consequences. One small thing – seemingly insignificant – can lead to something bigger which leads to something even bigger, and on and on it goes. Until one day, you look up and the BIG thing you wanted in life isn't done, because the daily small things (like the nail) didn't get done.

Adulting Like a Boss

Often the Hard Thing that comes later when we choose to do the easy thing – not tending to the nail – is what DOESN'T happen. It's that good thing that could have come if only we had tended to the Hard Thing in a timely manner.

But you! You're Adulting Like a Boss! You're doing the Hard Thing.

Chances are that you've suffered some of those Hard Things from taking the easy road. I know I sure have! I've procrastinated, ignored, and in-decisioned myself into hard places many times. It's through those experiences that I've learned the life lesson of doing the Hard Thing *now*, and getting the good stuff that follows.

> **Often the hard thing that comes later when we choose to do the easy thing — not tending to the nail — is what DOESN'T happen.**

A not-so-funny then but hilarious-now story

My very handy-man husband learned the lesson of doing the Hard Thing now and Adulting when it's easier to run from responsibility!

When we were first married, my hubby and I rented a cute condo, but it had a drippy faucet. Rather than asking our landlord to fix it, hubby decided to fix it himself. He had received a nice set of tools at his man-shower party, and he was eager to use the tools and impress his new wife.

So, he used the screwdriver and removed the handle of the dripping faucet.

Conclusion

Without turning the water off at its source first.

A geyser erupted the minute the faucet handle was unscrewed.

Did I mention it was the HOT water?

It shot up with such force that it was actually hitting the ceiling and raining down scalding hot water and bits of ceiling that were coming loose. All…thirty…gallons of HOT water.

Of course he immediately reached under the sink to turn the water off. Except, the handle under the sink was broken and you couldn't turn it off without a pair of pliers. Which he had left in the toolbox in the garage.

He left the bathroom, ran to the garage to get the pliers, and as he turned back toward the house, he thought to himself, "I just want to leave."

Sometimes when we find ourselves in a difficult situation, we'd rather just leave. Either leave physically (as in this case) or leave emotionally. But doing the Hard Thing is worth the work!

Hubby knew no one was coming to fix the problem; he knew it was up to him to fix it himself! And that was the day, he says, that he became a real Adult.

It's that moment you realize that you are the one who has to do this Hard Thing! If you don't do it, it won't get done at all, so you take your power pose, and do it! (And then Snapchat it to your friends so they know how cool you are for doing the Hard Thing!)

> **Sometimes when we find ourselves in a difficult situation, we'd rather just leave. But doing the hard thing is worth the work!**

What looked like freedom led to slavery. It's doing the Hard Thing now that leads to freedom. Freedom through responsibility, making good decisions, forming good relationships, taking care of yourself, and doing the Hard Thing. That's Adulting. Adulting Like a Boss.

END

Thank You for Reading My Book!

I appreciate all your feedback and love hearing what you have to say.

Will you take a moment to leave an honest review for this book on Amazon? Reviews are the BEST way others can find out about the book.

Thanks so much!

Laura Thomae Young

ACKNOWLEDGEMENTS

I am so grateful for my husband, Steve, who has not only been my encourager through this project, but also helped with formatting, layout, and other stuff that goes into making a book that I don't know how to do.

Thank you to the millennials in my life, starting with two of my very own, Mary Kathryn and Audrey, who were by my side through this journey. And to family and friends who believed in me, and cheered me on when I announced I was writing a book.

I'm indebted to those who participated in "the interview" I conducted for research. Thank you for inspiration, conversation, and answering zillions of my questions. I've loved the "Adulting Like a Boss" parties we've had at my house, and I've learned that a chocolate fountain is a great catalyst for forming new friendships.

I appreciate those who answered my many questions about real estate, mortgages, and taxes: Diane Hayes, Gigi Spires, Allison Hoadley, Greg Awbrey, Emmett Hennessey, and my mother-in-love, Estelle Sherer.

Thanks to Michelle Chalkey, my editor, who has been wonderful. I am grateful for the authors and podcasters who have taught me and inspired me: Hal Elrod, Pat Flynn, Jon Acuff, Chandler Bolt, Honorée Corder, Shane and Jocelyn Sams, Jen Sincero, Jeff Goins, and Gina Horkey. You made it seem that ordinary people could achieve their goals, and now I see that is true.

About the Author

Laura Thomae Young is a writer, workshop leader, and international speaker with more than twenty years of experience working with teens, young adults, and women.

The idea for the "Adulting Like a Boss" website and book came after her return from living abroad for more than a decade. Upon acclimating back to life in the States, she came across more and more friends in the upcoming generation who lacked confidence in tackling adult situations, both big and small.

Her passion for teaching and connecting with young adults prompted her to seek an avenue to equip millennials for the grown-up world. Thus, *Adulting Like a Boss* was born to provide the life skills needed to move from college student to grown-up.

She is a mom to four millennials of her own and mother-in-law to three. When she's not writing, training, or speaking, you'll find her hanging out at her home in Nashville with her husband, Steve, and their giant labradoodle, Val.

Made in the USA
Lexington, KY
25 October 2017